Words of Praise for *Unison Reading: Socially Group Instruction for Equity and Achievement*

"Professor McCallister has developed one of the most exciting and important educational innovations I have ever seen. In an era where schools are forced into a Faustian choice between time spent on academic skills and time spent on social, moral, and character development, along comes this ingenious program, a theoretical and practical breath of fresh air, which elegantly does it all at the same time. This book should be read by anyone interested in improving education."

Joshua Aronson, Associate Professor, New York University, New York, NY Editor, *Improving Academic Achievement: Impact of Psychological Factors on Education*

"Unison Reading offers the promise of an effective approach to reading instruction based on sound theory and a substantial body of research. It is a powerful antidote to the hyperfocus on low level reading skills that plagues reading instruction in urban schools and special education classrooms."

Curt Dudley-Marling, Professor of Education, Lynch School of Education, Boston College, Boston, MA

"Thank you, Cynthia McCallister, for this remarkable contribution to practices of collaborative learning. The concept of Unison Reading not only reminds us that learning is fundamentally a social process. Most helpfully, we are introduced to the fine details of how this process can increase motivation, attention, mutually supportive relationships, and reading mastery. I am much impressed, and we should all be grateful."

Kenneth J. Gergen, Senior Research Professor, Swarthmore College, Swarthmore, PA Author, *Relational Being, Beyond Self and Community*

"With the publication of *Unison Reading*, Cynthia McCallister reminds us to stop labeling children and to begin listening to them and learning from them. At the same time, she demonstrates through example, the importance of teachers and administrators becoming researchers in their own classrooms, ever on the lookout for new and powerful ways of working with diverse literacy learners. Above all, the author highlights the importance of camaraderie, respect and support as children learn to read in the company of their peers."

Shelley Harwayne, Former Superintendent, Community School District Two, Author and Educational Consultant, New York, NY

"Unison Reading provides practical benefits through the ability to scale high quality instruction. It enables educators to deliver the kind of attention to individual performance that is normally only attained through one-on-one instruction. The theoretically-grounded structures of Unison Reading get students talking with each other in a way that allows teachers to simultaneously concentrate on and evaluate teaching and learning. As a science education researcher I've used Unison Reading to hear students co-construct and talk about scientific words, claims, and evidence and found it to be a powerful tool to design transformative instruction."

Susan Kirch, Ph.D., Associate Professor, Science Education, Department of Teaching and Learning, New York University, Steinhardt School of Culture, Education and Human Development, New York, NY

"Unison Reading makes a space for a unique kind of synergy between student learning and teacher learning. This carefully structured (but not scripted) design enables teachers to inquire into diverse literacy learners' understandings and use of prior experience and knowledge just as these learners are themselves trusted and afforded agency to search for meaningful ideas and connections, not simply for facts or right answers. McCallister and her colleagues in schools have spawned an enormously generative idea that creates a lively and inclusive learning environment. For teachers who want to make their practice a very rich context for learning about students' learning—in order to teach them better—this approach provides a remarkable opportunity."

Susan Lytle, Ph.D., Professor of Education, Director of the Programs in Reading/ Writing/Literacy, Graduate School of Education, University of Pennsylvania

"I know how hard it is to challenge received wisdom about teaching and learning. All of what I've called educational common sense supports the failed status quo. Cynthia McCallister's *Unison Reading* boldly proposes and shows how to achieve a deep change of theory and practice in one of the most studied and still dogmatically entrenched areas of schooling: the acquisition and development of reading. It promises to live up to its subtitle and build socially inclusive classrooms producing equity and achievement. And, most exciting of all, this uncommon sense approach will banish boredom and bring joy and excitement back to the reading class as all children work together to make meaning from the texts they are sharing."

John S. Mayher, Professor Emeritus, English Education, New York University

"If we want to create a truly democratic society where people have the skills to freely exchange ideas, then our schools need to model a more democratic reading instruction process. Unison Reading allows us to do this by teaching students what they need without segregating them into groups based solely on ability. For more than a 100 years, small group reading instruction has been taught in U.S. schools by creating a hierarchy of leveled groups, all of which has done nothing to close the achievement gap, and probably contributed to reinforcing it. As the principal who collaborated with McCallister to pilot the implementation of Unison Reading on a Pre-K–8 schoolwide basis, I have witnessed first hand its true power to dramatically raise reading achievement. Growth of students in all grades outpaced the national norm, and the rates of achievement in our lowest performing students have been even more dramatic. Unison Reading, if brought to a larger scale, can close the achievement gap."

Kerry Rutishauser, Principal, The Jacob Riis School—P.S. 126/Manhattan Academy of Technology, New York City Department of Education, New York, NY

"Unison Reading could be the most innovative approach to reading instruction that I've come across in the last 20 years. It has the potential to transform classroom practice, enabling students to meet the highest quality standards of reading instruction. A must-read."

Susan B. Neuman, Professor of Educational Studies, University of Michigan, Ann Arbor, MI, and Former U.S. Assistant Secretary of Elementary and Secondary Education

unison
READING

For Packie, Fiona, and Liam

unison
READING

Socially Inclusive Group Instruction for Equity and Achievement

Cynthia McCallister

Foreword by **David R. Olson**
Afterword by **Edmund W. Gordon**

CORWIN
A SAGE Company

For information:

Corwin
A SAGE Company
2455 Teller Road
Thousand Oaks, California 91320
(800) 233-9936
Fax: (800) 417-2466
www.corwin.com

SAGE Ltd.
1 Oliver's Yard
55 City Road
London EC1Y 1SP
United Kingdom

SAGE India Pvt. Ltd.
B 1/I 1 Mohan Cooperative
    Industrial Area
Mathura Road, New Delhi 110 044
India

SAGE Asia-Pacific Pte. Ltd.
33 Pekin Street #02-01
Far East Square
Singapore 048763

Printed in the United States of America

Library of Congress Cataloging-in-Publication Data

McCallister, Cynthia, date
Unison reading : socially inclusive group instruction for equity and achievement / Cynthia McCallister.
    p. cm.
Includes bibliographical references and index.
ISBN 978-1-4129-8664-9 (pbk.)

   1. Group reading—United States. 2. Educational equalization—United States. 3. Language arts (Elementary)—United States. I. Title.

LC6651.M33 2011
372.41'64—dc22   2010029358

This book is printed on acid-free paper.

10 11 12 13 14   10 9 8 7 6 5 4 3 2 1

Acquisitions Editor:	Carol Chambers Collins
Editorial Assistant:	Sarah Bartlett
Production Editor:	Cassandra Margaret Seibel
Copy Editor:	Nancy Conger
Typesetter:	C&M Digitals (P) Ltd.
Proofreader:	Jennifer Gritt
Indexer:	Terri Corry
Cover Designer:	Scott Van Atta
Permissions Editor:	Adele Hutchinson

Contents

Additional materials and resources from the author may be found at www.unisonreading.com.

List of Figures

Foreword

For educators, these general principles have long been clear:

1. Children learn best through trying and undergoing rather than through listening or through prescriptive drills.

2. Children learn not only with others but through others, through discourse, and through the sharing and comparing of beliefs.

3. Written language is embedded in and is an extension of oral speech, and structure is acquired in the context of function.

4. Even in the context of the most enabling teacher, it is still the child who does the learning and who must ultimately become responsible for that learning.

5. It is not only the teacher and the society that judges the student's work by assigning praise and blame but the child and his or her classmates that must be able, in the longer term, to make the judgment as to whether or not a performance has met some acceptable standard.

6. The school plays a critical role in integrating children into learning communities rather than separating them into streams with divergent futures.

Progressive educators have long held these principles, but successes to put them into practice have not been sufficiently impressive to challenge the entrenched traditional methods: setting specific goals, teaching to them, testing the students, assigning praise and blame, and reward and punishment. Indeed, even the recently updated version of No Child Left Behind (NCLB) adopts this traditional teaching-testing format, merely adding more carrots and whips, prizes and threats. The traditional methods survive in part through an unwarranted narrowing of the goals: namely, to those goals that are easily stated, for which materials are profitably manufactured and published, and achievements readily monitored through tests. Only as an afterthought do other goals—such as developing the students' ability to make cognitive and moral judgments—come to be mentioned, and the goal of developing student's ability to take responsibility for aspects of their own learning and behavior is overlooked entirely.

It is for these reasons that McCallister's program, described in this volume, offers something new and exciting to the practice of education. All of the principles mentioned above are exemplified in the activity she calls Unison Reading: the practice of allowing small, diverse groups of children to read together orally and to stop and discuss what happened when individual readings diverge. Reading resumes when the local difficulty is resolved. In Unison Reading, learning is collaborative: That is, the children share their understandings and misunderstanding with others, and resolving those differences is what promotes learning. Students take on responsibility not only for deciding what text to read and with whom to read it, but also for judging when they or someone else understands or misunderstands, succeeds or fails. Reading is not primarily a matter of learning the rules of phonology but rather of learning to use language for a number of important social purposes such as persuading others, offering information, enticing others to share an interest, reporting, and criticizing. Phonological issues involved in word and sentence reading are addressed when they arise, rather than as part of a linear, prescribed program. Nor is the program dictated by the mandates of the publishers and curriculum designers, but rather by the expressed interests, goals, and problems of the learners themselves; materials are readily found in the highly literate environments of the community and the school. Most importantly, accountability is conspicuous throughout the program. Not only are children tested with standardized tests as the state requires, but accountability is distributed through the learning system. Accountability, we may say, begins at home. The children themselves are not only given opportunity for taking on responsibilities for their own learning and actions, they learn to judge when and whether they have met those responsibilities.

Carrots and sticks have been proven more effective with mules than children. As critics note, rewards and punishment are as likely to produce "stupefied acquiescence" as they are to produce genuine learning. The accountability that matters is that which develops as children learn to take responsibility for their own learning and their own actions and when they help others to make judgments about theirs.

How does the program Unison Reading accomplish all this? Both the art of teaching and the organization of the classroom and the school change importantly, as McCallister's account describes. In essence, there is a basic appreciation that literacy is primarily an extension of using language for sharing experience on a one-to-one basis rather than on the more usual impersonal "broadcast" mode typical of whole-class teaching. The program amplifies children's opportunities for speaking and for speaking to attentive others about the texts they are writing and reading and for clarifying misunderstandings in the process. It offers children boundless opportunities for speaking, changing the classroom from one where listening and remembering are primary to a classroom where speaking to others about what they are reading is the focus. Misreadings and misunderstandings come up for discussion, offering opportunities for grasping ideas and sharing epiphanies. It takes a bold teacher to recognize that children may learn new ideas, such as the difference between "suspecting" and "believing," just through talk with others, rather than through definitions offered by the teacher. Most of us have an irrepressible urge to teach. McCallister's classrooms prove that—not always of course, but to a remarkable and previously unacknowledged extent—children in groups often arrive at the correct solutions, by themselves. That is how they learn to take responsibility for their own learning, to know when they understand or don't understand. In the process they are acquiring the sense of responsibility that the traditional model of teaching and testing either ignored completely or delegated to something loosely called "moral education."

Many of the principles that underlie McCallister's work are supported by the contemporary research programs described in Preiss and Sternberg's (2010) *Innovations in Educational Psychology: Perspectives on Learning, Teaching and Human Development*. These principles include the importance of building on what children already know implicitly, small-group discussion between the children themselves in arriving at new knowledge, learning to make judgments about one's own and other's work and of learning the standards involved in making those judgments, and children's agency and responsibility. Unison Reading offers a format for implementing these principles. If the dramatic effects so far shown by early testing results continue to demonstrate the effectiveness of Unison Reading and its pedagogical underpinnings, Progressives may at last have a viable alternative to the teaching and testing, the carrot and stick model of education, that has dominated research and practice for a century.

David R. Olson
OISE/University of Toronto

Preface

Unison Reading defines reading as a fundamentally social experience in which the meaning that an individual makes of a text reaches its full potential through a collective experience. This is common sense for most people outside of schools, where the underlying purpose of the social situation determines how we read and what we make of texts. Whether we're scanning menus or subway maps, studying textbooks or religious texts, or reading income tax instructions, we often consult with others to determine what meaning we should make of texts and how those meanings should shape our actions and understandings. All authentic reading—or reading that we do with real purpose—is shaped by the intentions, goals, and beliefs we bring to the larger task at hand. But the history of reading instruction, with its focus on best practices and balanced instruction, has nearly always concentrated on which aspects of the text to emphasize in *teaching*. Should teachers emphasize the process of meaning making or the particular cognitive skills involved in reading? The persistent debate over the relative merits of instruction that emphasizes *skills* over instruction that emphasizes *meaning* is familiar to most teachers of reading. In the field of reading instruction, the parameters of this debate are set by a conventional understanding that reading is a process that involves one person in the act of deciphering a text to achieve meaning.

While it is true that reading is ultimately a process of making meaning from symbols, it is also a commonsense fact that the very essence of what meanings are made in the act of reading has everything to do with the reader's subjective experiences. It is also true that it is a peculiarly human capacity that allows us, through social experiences, to engage with others and think about things from the perspective of what they might be thinking about those things. These intersubjective experiences allow us to expand and deepen our personal understanding. These insights play out in our relationships with others and are fundamental to the process of reading and learning to read. When reading teachers overlook the relational dimensions of pedagogical situations and the subjective experiences they cultivate—as traditional reading methods have tended to do—they miss opportunities to nurture the most significant dimensions of the act of reading through children's connections to their peers.

Unison Reading is based on the belief that the reader's intentions are every bit as significant to the experience of reading as the features of the texts themselves and that interactions with others play a pivotal role in shaping intentions. Children's intentions and the social interactions that foster them deserve strong emphasis in instruction. The term *unison* in the name of this approach recognizes the idea that reading is fundamentally a social process and that children best acquire desired dispositions as readers in the company of others. The Unison Reading protocol creates a communal situation in which children can learn from one another.

This book responds to a demand for reading instruction that provides children with opportunities to integrate multiple skills and strategies in the context of authentic reading experiences. There have been recent calls to end the intractable debate about how best to teach reading by suggesting that skills and meaning should be balanced through an *integrated* approach to the teaching of reading. While this view recognizes that good reading instruction combines attention to letter-sound relationships with an emphasis on meaning, the locus of integration is typically within the teacher's instructional plan. Unison Reading presses the point that it is the reader's interaction with the text that dictates which reading cues deserve attention. So far, what has been lacking is an approach to reading instruction that places the locus of integration with the *child* rather than the teacher. Unison Reading is a method that shifts responsibility to children for determining which information sources to attend to during the reading process and how these should be integrated.

Unison Reading is also based on a commitment to social justice. Ironically, in spite of over 50 years of commitment to racial integration in schools since the U.S. Supreme Court's decision in *Brown v. Board of Education,* common instructional practices such as leveled reading groups (or ability groups) still continue to function as sorting mechanisms within the classroom. These practices establish and secure patterns of inequality that mirror inequities found outside of school.

Unison Reading interrupts this cycle by defining literacy as an outcome of a reader's participation in widening circles of social experience that foster new cognitive competencies. Based on the Vygotskiian principle that understanding often develops first within the social context before being internalized as a private psychological skill, Unison Reading involves all members of a small group in a joint oral reading of the same text. This process brings to communal consciousness any aspect of the text that caused confusion for one of its members and allows for critical analysis and understanding. Ability groups are abandoned together with the notion that knowledge can be transmitted from teacher to student through a linear sequence of skills to be practiced and mastered. Instead, children are integrated into groups based on interest in texts that they themselves have chosen—groups of common interests and varied talents. Children with comparatively limited or delayed reading literacy enjoy a strong scaffold of support for their participation, and higher-functioning readers have opportunities to foster critical comprehension.

During its piloting as the schoolwide reading program in a Pre-K–8 Title I school in Manhattan, Unison Reading was associated with dramatic gains in reading achievement. After one year of implementation, the average rate of growth of students at every level in the school from second to eighth grade, outpaced the national average rate of growth on the Degrees of Reading Power assessment, the progress monitoring system used in the school. These gains are addressed fully in the Conclusion section of this book. I hope one major message this book delivers is that equity is more than a lofty democratic ideal. When classrooms exemplify the values of democratic society, children flourish.

Unison Reading has grown out of a broader pedagogical approach that I have developed over two decades as a teacher and researcher, which I call Genre Practice.[1] This progressive approach to literacy pedagogy is founded on the idea that children are naturally inclined to grow and learn, and that schooling should nurture these instincts while at the same time providing all children with sufficient opportunity to learn what society expects them to learn. It is based on the belief that children learn most when they have freedom to read and write texts of their choosing, to collaborate with peers of their choice, to hold themselves accountable to high learning standards, to size up their own strengths and needs, and to make commitments to things they need to improve upon.

Founded on the idea that school should enhance children's flourishing and well being, Unison Reading and other Genre Practice methods are designed to instill confidence, pride, and a sense of engagement in children. These aims have roots in my own vivid memories of primary school, sitting beside my beloved first-grade teacher, Mrs. Wise, during our regular Round Robin reading lessons. The intense feelings of existential discomfort I experienced during these meetings are etched into my memory: I can see myself in my mind's eye, face flushed, palms sweating, heart racing, and intently focused on trying to identify the place in the text when it would be my turn to read aloud, alone, to my group, exposed to their critical scrutiny. Though I learned how to read, I also

---

[1]Genrepractice.org was created as a source of information for those interested in learning more about the Genre Practice model. Visit genrepractice.org to learn more.

learned to dislike reading. My reading competence was achieved at the cost of my compromised sense of identity as a reader. Those early memories turned into gut-level instincts about the generative power of positive school experiences.

Unison Reading transforms what, for many children, are alienating and tedious routines into pleasurable and engaging social rituals. Unison Reading is an antidote to the humiliating and soul crushing methods of old, and strives to support flourishing and well being in children. But perhaps more importantly, the Unison Reading method provides a method for teachers to support the mission of literacy development as means for children to begin to access their basic civil and human rights. In his speech commemorating International Literacy Day, U.N. Secretary General Kofi Annan (2009) stated,

> Literacy is essential to the development and health of individuals, communities, and countries. It is a condition for people's effective participation in the democratic process. It is the basis for the written communication and literature that have long provided the main channel for cross-cultural awareness and understanding. And, at the same time, it is the most precious way we have of expressing, preserving, and developing our cultural diversity and identity. Literacy, in short, is a prerequisite for peace.

More than the acquisition of reading and writing skills, literacy is a means through which children learn to take from and participate in their culture. Founded upon the principle that reading is a cultural practice, the Unison Reading method provides a context for children to exercise their rights and responsibilities as citizens.

About This Book

This book resulted from my extensive work with the faculty of the Jacob Riis School, a public Pre-K–8 Title I school in Manhattan, New York City, where Unison Reading was adopted as the primary method of group instruction for children of all grades. In a sense, these teachers' probing questions have contributed to the framework for this book, and my responses have become the content. The teachers who became skilled at Unison Reading—so much so that they taught me a thing or two about the approach—are featured in this book to offer examples of Unison Reading practice.

This book is written as a guide to help teachers who are interested in implementing Unison Reading in their classrooms and schools. It presents Unison Reading as both a method and a program, including practical guidance and solid theoretical support. Chapter 1 provides an overarching introduction to Unison Reading, briefly explaining the method and principles and providing you with enough information to begin to experiment with Unison Reading. Chapter 2 provides a detailed account of the system of practices that will enable you to successfully implement Unison Reading as a classroomwide instructional program.

Once you have implemented Unison Reading in your classroom, you will more than likely be convinced of its potential to support all children's reading development, but you may still have some questions. Chapter 3 provides a deeper explanation of the underlying principles of Unison Reading and sets it in a context of other conventional reading instruction approaches.

Chapter 4 presents narrative accounts by teachers who have used Unison Reading in their classrooms. Through these narratives, many frequently asked questions are addressed, such as how can Unison Reading meet the needs of both delayed and advanced readers in mixed-ability groups? How are skills and strategies taught when children select their own texts and determine the course of instruction? How can Unison Reading meet the needs of English language learners or children with special needs?

Unison Reading is a novel approach to reading instruction based on some concepts inspired by theories that haven't made their way into mainstream traditional reading pedagogy. Because my intention is to introduce new ideas, it is unavoidable to use the terms that represent them. In cases where I use terms not typically associated with conventional reading practices, I provide definitions in glossary boxes.

Unison Reading is a generative pedagogy for teachers and students alike. Everyone who participates in a Unison Reading group has an opportunity to learn and grow. Because the locus of new learning springs from within the group—not from external curriculum sources—all participants gain more insight and literally get smarter as a byproduct of social participation in Unison Reading groups. Teachers learn to listen to the ways in which children make sense of their reading and to record their insights, and children learn to listen not only to their peers as a source of new learning, but to themselves in order to clarify their own thinking. Unison Reading offers a way for children and teachers alike to step out of the constraints of age-old tradition and to do things differently.

Acknowledgments

U nison Reading is the product of many years of research and collaboration and many people deserve credit for its development.

Founded on Progressive educational philosophy and pedagogical traditions, the wisdom of John Dewey, Maria Montessori, and Sylvia Ashton Warner find expression in this book. The psychological theories of Piaget, Vygotsky, Bruner, and David Olson are also foundational to Unison Reading. This work is also the product of two decades of my own internal dialog between the competing discourses of social and cultural psychology mingled with practitioner pedagogical theory in an ongoing argument with the general psychology of reading. The voices in this dialog are too numerous to credit here, but the pages of Unison Reading pay homage to a wide range of theoretical and philosophical intellectual traditions that deserve recognition.

Kerry Decker Rutishauser, the visionary principal of the Jacob Riis School in Manhattan, is a kindred spirit to whom I owe a deep debt of gratitude. Her abiding faith in progressive education, her commitment to education as a tool for social justice and educational equity, her intelligence, courage, humility, fortitude, and plain pioneer grit were the requisite traits that enabled Unison Reading to be successfully implemented in a large Pre-K–8 school in Manhattan that serves a population of over 750 children. Despite all possible odds that might have otherwise extinguished successful reform, Kerry fearlessly tackled every obstacle in order to ensure that Unison Reading was successfully implemented. She saw the powerful potential of Unison Reading as a means to support literacy development for all children, and by involving me in her uncompromising effort to improve her school and to provide every child with an education that is personally meaningful and rigorous, she gave me the opportunity to refine the concept and protocol for Unison Reading in the company of a community of culturally and linguistically diverse children.

The teachers at the Jacob Riis School are the muses of Unison Reading. While it was I who initially taught them the Unison Reading protocol, they brought the approach to life in their classrooms, invited me to join in their reading groups, and showed me its true potential. Special thanks goes to Ede Blabac, Lauren Casion, Anna-Liisa Corsi, Jaime Disken, Filippa Ferriolo, Priscilla Fields, Rachel Goren, Barry Greenberg, Laura Ingram, Maria Ioannou, Meredith Jacks, Emily Jarrell, Jaela Kim, Bethan Kovach, Rachel Kovach, Ian Lambert, Isabel Lee, Susan Lesser, Sari Marder, Sabina McNamara, Shara Miller, Lillian Ng., Karen Parker, Chris Piccigallo, Amy Piller, Ariel Ricciardi, Darleen Rosado, Elisa Sansone, Erin Scutt, Adrianne Shultis, Ilene Silverman, Becky Terrigno, Rosario Then, Stephanie Ward, Mei Yi Wong, Lauren Wren, and Lisa Yun-Wong. I'd also like to thank Robin Berg and Carlos Romero, the assistant principals of the Jacob Riis School, for their invaluable assistance in implementing Unison Reading. I would also like to express gratitude to Margaret Javor and the office staff for all their support.

David Olson has been a source of guidance and inspiration throughout the evolution of this book. A widely renowned and respected cultural psychologist, his scholarship in psychological development, literacy theory, and his theory of responsibility became my compass in the evolution of Unison Reading. His generosity as a friend and partner in ongoing conversations about the psychology of learning, pedagogical practices, and the central aims of education not only helped sharpen my ideas, but instilled in me a sense of confidence in holding them.

Edmund Gordon was a generous teacher who, as my mentor through the Spencer Foundation's Scholar Development Program, welcomed me into his home and helped me think about teaching and learning through the lens of cultural psychology. I thank him especially for that memorable afternoon sitting in his study in the spring of 1998 when he pressed me to name the phenomenon that was at the heart of the approach to instruction I was developing. I mumbled in response, *intentionality?* And my fate for the next decade was sealed as I devoted myself to developing Unison Reading, a pedagogy of intentionality. Unison Reading is also a pedagogy of equity, and Ed deserves credit for helping me consider and apply the principles of equality and justice into my work. Ed's voice continues to be a constant reminder that educational opportunities are only equal when all children have what they need in order to succeed.

Jerome Bruner is an iconic scholar whose work on early language acquisition and the cultural processes of education shaped the contours of the practices described in this book. Jerry is also a generous neighbor and NYU colleague who has gracefully obliged my occasional impositions to read drafts of my ideas and indulged me in conversations that are consistently enlightening and always leave an impact on my thinking.

Unison Reading involves careful observation of children, and I'd like to give a word of thanks to Jim Rog, a close personal friend who was also one of my first professors as a doctoral student. Jim was a demanding teacher who showed me how to apply rigorous ethnographic methods to classroom observation. Through his teaching I learned how careful observation of children could provide powerful insights into practice.

I would also like to thank Carol Collins, my editor at Corwin, who made a strong enough case that there was a market for a book that reconceptualized reading as primarily a social process. I'd like to also thank Susan Liddicoat, whose careful reading and editing of the book helped smooth the jagged edges of my ideas on paper. Jackie Aiello is my trusted research assistant, whose hard work, generosity, and commitment to this project helped it come to fruition.

This book would not have ever come about had it not been for my own children. Unison Reading is my solution to deeply dysfunctional educational practices that I witnessed through my own children's educational experiences. My youngest son, Liam, has had the opportunity to take part in Unison Reading first-hand as a student enrolled at the Jacob Riis School. One late evening, when we'd left homework a little too long and he still had reading to do, he appealed to me, "Wanna unison read with me, Mommy?" This and other countless moments confirmed that the instructional practices I had a hand in developing were proving their worth. He minimized the isolation of writing a book by making the work seem more personally relevant and its warrant more immediate and necessary.

Finally, without Gerry Rooney, my husband, and soul mate, this book, and so many other things that matter most to me, would never have been possible. He is my first editor and most honest critic. Words don't do justice to the gratitude and appreciation I hold for his countless sacrifices, unending patience, and tolerance for our lives to be consumed by the work that led to the culmination of this book.

PUBLISHER'S ACKNOWLEDGMENTS   ■

Corwin gratefully acknowledges the contributions of the following reviewers:

Kathryn Abels, EC Resource Teacher
Bishop Spaugh Community Academy
Charlotte, NC

Cindy Ballenger, Early Childhood Specialist
Chèche Konnen Center—TERC

Judy Brunner, Clinical Faculty and Chief Education Officer
Missouri State University and Instructional Solutions Group
Springfield, MO

Wendy Caszatt-Allen, Middle School Teacher
Mid-Prairie Community School District
Kalona, IA

Christy A. Heid, Associate Professor of Education and Science
Chatham University
Pittsburgh, PA

Dolores Hennessy, Reading Specialist
New Milford Public Schools
New Milford, CT

Joan Irwin, Professional Development Consultant
Newark, DE

Charity Jennings, Full-Time Faculty
Department of Education
University of Phoenix
Phoenix, AZ

Karen Kozy-Landress, Speech/Language Pathologist
MILA Elementary School
Merritt Island, FL

Cindy Kratzer, Director
Sierra Educational Consulting
Marina del Rey, CA

Sharon Latimer, ESL Pre-K Teacher
Parker, TX

Charre Todd, Science Instructor Facilitator
Norman Middle School
Crossett, AR

Randy Wormald, High School Teacher/Technology Integrator
Belmont High School
Belmont, NH

About the Author

Cynthia McCallister is the creator of Unison Reading, a method for group reading instruction that conceives of reading first and foremost as a form of social activity through which particular skills and competencies develop. Cynthia developed Unison Reading over two decades in her roles as a teacher-practitioner and a scholar. During her early professional life as a teacher of young children, Cynthia became intrigued by how readily children mastered reading and writing in the context of activities that made literacy engaging and playful. And throughout her experiences as a mother of three children in New York City public schools, a K–5 teacher (in rural Maine and New York City), a teacher educator, staff developer, and school reformer with extensive involvement in a wide range of culturally and linguistically diverse Pre-K–8 schools, Cynthia has come to understand that learning for every child depends on engagement, curiosity, a personal commitment to the objects of learning, and an opportunity to acquire new ideas in the company of others.

Cynthia is an Associate Professor at New York University, where she is the founding director of the program in Literacy Education. She received her doctoral degree from the University of Maine in 1995.

Learn more about Unison Reading by visiting unisonreading.com. You can also learn more about the Genre Practice method by visiting genrepractice.org.

1

What Is Unison Reading?

The Method

"It's like we're one—A team!" is the way Aaron, a sixth-grade boy, explained the practice of Unison Reading to a group of teachers visiting his classroom. His is an apt description. Unison Reading involves two to five children together in coordinated reading of a common text with a few simple rules: Synchronize your reading by actually saying the words aloud in unison; listen to one another—that means you have to speak softly enough to make sure you can hear one another; stop the group when you don't understand a word or an idea (as opposed to the teacher stopping the group at a preplanned point in the text for the purpose of premeditated instruction); and be promotive and supportive of everyone in the group. Unison Reading creates a sequence of student-initiated pauses that serve as spaces for discussion about text features and ideas, allowing a child experiencing confusion to benefit from the insights of several other perspectives. Unison Reading is based on the principle that understanding is often first socially acquired before being internalized as a personal cognitive skill. Unison Reading involves all members of a small group taking part in a singular reading of the same text, affording the opportunity for the group to critically consider features of the text or the reading process that deserve attention.

This chapter is intended to provide an explanation of the Unison Reading method so that you can gain enough confidence to immediately try it in your classroom. I provide basic information on Unison Reading procedures and explain how to use the Unison Reading Record. Extended examples offer evidence from real classrooms of students' growth as readers through this approach.

UNISON READING: A PEDAGOGICAL REVOLUTION

Unison Reading is an innovative approach to instruction that is revolutionary in important ways:

• *Unison Reading maximizes the opportunity children have to communicate and learn from others.* Unison Reading redefines group reading instruction around the understanding that reading is as much a social experience characterized by **intermental** abilities, as it is an individual cognitive experience defined strictly by **intramental** abilities. Cultural psychologists, like Vygotsky and his supporters, maintain that higher-order cognitive abilities develop through opportunities to participate with others in cultural group experiences. Of course, children have always learned things as a result of participating in the social routines of school. But in the context of traditional reading instruction, where the development of individual cognitive competencies have been the focus of attention, interpersonal relational processes have been relatively neglected for their potential to promote learning. Unison Reading is an approach that rests on the understanding that much of what we know about reading is learned through cultural transmission and emphasizes, as Ruth Benedict (1934) suggested, the "enormous role of the cultural process of transmission" above the "small scope of the biological" (p. 150). The logic behind Unison Reading is that social situations, like the instructional reading group, can be carefully organized to give rise to desired cognitive abilities. Unison Reading attends as carefully to cultural transmission as it does to cognitive transmission, not only tending to the cognitive factors that are commonly the focus of conventional reading instruction approaches, but also to the social competencies and interpersonal behaviors that are required of literate individuals across the diversity of social contexts. These competencies are as vital to the process of reading as decoding and comprehension, which have traditionally dominated the focus of group reading instruction. In Unison Reading groups, children engage in what Jerome Bruner called "bootstrapping" (1996) by sharing insights and helping one another. These instances of bootstrapping exploit the capacity of group members to share and collaborate for mutual benefit.

GLOSSARY BOX: INTERMENTAL

of or relating to psychological abilities that originate in relationships with others

GLOSSARY BOX: INTRAMENTAL

of or relating to cognitive processes that occur within the person

• *Unison Reading is a pragmatic approach to instruction that emphasizes the functionality of reading in addition to skills mastery and reading accuracy.* When children participate in reading groups, not only are they learning to master the skills of reading, they are learning how to use established communicative conventions to take part in the "speech act" patterns of their cultures. The Unison Reading method is premised on the understanding that literacy competencies arise through communicative use and functional appropriateness. The program is designed to contrast with the more traditional approach to literacy development that emphasizes the accumulation and assessment of basic skills under the direction of the teacher within the context of a rigidly applied program. Rather than teaching the conventions of reading in a linear, systematic manner—the conventional approach to the reading curriculum with a long tradition—Unison Reading is organized around routinized social situations that provide children ongoing opportunities to learn how to assume an active stance in relation to the text at hand. Through active involvement with others, as they exercise their reading stance, children learn the conventions of reading. A caveat: Unison Reading rejects the notion that children learn what they need to learn naturally by merely being engaged in social reading situations, a common criticism of child-centered approaches. Rather, the Unison Reading routine is structured around a fixed system of rules and expectations that hold children accountable to learning standards and group norms.

• *The Unison Reading protocol redistributes responsibility for learning from the teacher to the students.* Teachers are no longer solely responsible for selecting texts, planning lessons, and facilitating groups. Students themselves acquire greater responsibility for their learning.

Students are no longer merely responsible for taking part in teacher-directed activities, the focus of traditional group instruction, but now have responsibility for selecting their own texts, facilitating group discussions, and managing their own learning. Unison Reading reconfigures the social order of group instruction because the authority for covering content is shifted from the teacher to the students, investing them with significant responsibility to determine what aspects of the text require attention in the context of instruction. Teaching is no longer a process of simply *telling* but successfully *facilitating* joint intentions and mutual understanding through dialog.

   • *Learning is organized around children's self-chosen interests and goals rather than around traditional ability groups.* Children have autonomy to make choices about which texts to read and which groups to join. This autonomy enhances motivation and engagement. Because the children themselves make choices about which groups to join based on interest, multi-ability groups form naturally. This method establishes a system for every child to have the opportunity to receive and to take from all others a central tenet of democratic education (Dewey, 1944). And by eliminating ability grouping, Unison Reading honors the democratic principle of the free exchange of ideas and integrates the classroom by inviting children to organize themselves into groups based on reading interest as opposed to ability. Groups are ideally comprised of children with a diverse range of competencies and experiences. In fact, Unison Reading *depends* on diversity within groups to reap the potential advantages in situations where each person brings unique and different strengths, needs, and perspectives. A simple discussion protocol gives children just enough structure to function independently. Once they have the freedom to decide for themselves what confuses or interests them, the rules of Unison Reading function to support collective conversations.

Unison Reading invites children to have conversations on what Vygotsky called the intermental plane, where each child's individual perspectives are clarified through collective dialog. The experience of reading texts together, so that collective questions and insights insinuate themselves into discussion, is good for all children. It provides a strong scaffold for children with comparatively limited or delayed reading literacy, allowing them to participate in the reading processes of more proficient readers. But it is equally advantageous to high-functioning readers, who benefit from extensive opportunities to refine existing competencies and develop higher-order thinking through deliberative dialog.

As children talk about their respective understandings, they both contribute to and gain from what is essentially a collective reading process. Unison Reading rules serve as a built-in mechanism that helps children develop and revise their thinking in reference to the way that others in their groups think. Individual understanding develops through opportunities to talk about letters, sounds, symbols, ideas, and even personal behaviors in reference to the way that others in their groups think about these things. This group process helps each individual child establish and secure generative reading behaviors and, ultimately, become more independent readers. Figure 1.1 summarizes the advantages of Unison Reading.

Figure 1.1 Advantages of Unison Reading

- Confers responsibility to students to identify points of confusion
- Addresses points of confusion explicitly and immediately in the context of the reading process
- Eliminates ability grouping (a practice proven to be detrimental to minority students' academic achievement)
- Dramatically increases the quantity of individual texts students read in instructional groups each year (30–40 per year in Unison Reading groups alone)
- Dramatically increases the number of social groups in which students are members
- Increases motivation by supporting autonomy (children get to select which texts to read), competence (group process generates ongoing behavioral feedback), and relatedness to others (groups are highly social)

■ THE UNISON READING METHOD

Unison Reading is a method of small-group reading instruction designed to be integrated into a larger reading curriculum. In a typical hour-long reading block, Unison Reading occupies only about 15–20 minutes of a student's time, four days a week.

During Unison Reading, children sit together in a circle, preferably at a small table, and read aloud together, in unison, multiple copies of the same text. Unison Reading groups typically consist of three to five students and a teacher. Groups should comprise no more than five children because children need to be able to hear and attend to each of their peers' oral reading and be close enough to point in to reference features of other group members' texts.

The Unison Reading rules are simple:

1. Read in sync with the others (don't read ahead because you'll confuse your group).

2. Read audibly so that others can hear you.

3. Be accountable to the group by speaking up when you're confused or curious about a word or an idea—these are valuable learning opportunities.

4. Be helpful and supportive to group members.

The last rule is the "golden rule" of Unison Reading. Everyone has the right to be treated with consideration and respect, and it is every person's responsibility to ensure similar treatment for others. Though the golden rule has roots in all major religions and is the foundation of the very concept of human rights, schools are too often a breeding ground for uncivil behaviors in children simply because conventional instructional practices don't incorporate civility as a significant instructional factor or address behavior infractions explicitly. Daily reading groups become a context in which children learn to be promotive in their interactions with peers. This rule exists not merely as a matter of good etiquette alone. Since knowledge traverses the relational pathways between people, social competencies and civility are essential pathways to mutual understanding and must be cultivated. All rules are posted in every classroom (see Figure 1.2).

Figure 1.2	Unison Reading Rules From Ariel Ricciardi and Jaime Disken's Fourth-Grade Classroom

Unison Reading Rules:
- Read in sync with the others
- Read audibly so that others can hear you
- Be accountable to the group by speaking up when you're confused by a word or an idea—these are valuable learning opportunities
- Be helpful and supportive to group members

Another rule that sixth-grade teacher Sabina McNamara adds to the protocol is this: Don't be bored! She holds her students accountable for being engaged and contributing to a group learning experience that is interesting.

For important reasons, Unison Reading is a rule-bound practice. Specific rules and expectations that govern group size, discourse patterns, and interpersonal support provide a scaffold to support agency and involvement. These rules create a container for social interaction that allows children with varying levels of sociocognitive competence to participate in and maintain cohesive learning groups. Once children become familiar with the simple ground rules, they can facilitate groups independently of the teacher, and many children readily choose the method of Unison Reading with a partner as a choice during independent reading time. Once they learn to abide by the rules of Unison Reading, even the youngest children are able to sustain relatively cohesive groups, even in the absence of their teacher. And once children learn to take responsibility for one another's behaviors by adhering to the rules, even children who exhibit challenging behaviors are kept in check by their peers.

Breaches: Opening Dialog to Support Literacy Learning

First, the group determines when and where to begin reading—shall we read the title first? Captions? The introduction or first paragraph? Typically, each group has a leader, a role that usually falls to the person who selected the text (which is usually not the teacher). The group leader gets the group started by saying something like, "Where shall we start reading?" Or, if the starting point is obvious, the ubiquitous, "Is everyone ready?" or, "One, two, three, go" (or, as Andreas jokes when it's his turn to be leader: "*Uno, dos, quatro . . .*" (in English, *one, two, four . . .*). As the group reads, the teacher typically joins in, careful not to lead with his or her voice or to dominate the group process (the point in Unison Reading is to participate, not to model).

Then, during the reading process, each child is expected to speak up when they don't understand or when they want to learn more. Children are taught that the group's learning potential is only as strong as each member's willingness to contribute to the dialog. Each child's confusions, missteps, understandings, or misunderstandings—what we refer to in Unison Reading as *breaches*—become points of discussion and instruction. In its form as a noun, a *breach* is a gap, opening, or break in something. Also a verb, *to make a breach* means to be the agent in the process of opening or breaking. In Unison Reading, breaches occur when unfamiliar words are encountered, but they also occur when sparks of curiosity fly, distracting behaviors interfere with the reading process, laughter erupts, or rules are broken (such as reading ahead or not reading out loud). We call these "breaches" because they are opportunities to break from reading in order to discuss ideas that arise from reading. Sixth-grade teacher Sabina McNamara lets her students know there are two types: "ah-ha!" breaches, and "huh?" breaches, and both open up important learning opportunities for the group.

Breaches essentially break open the reading process to create spaces or gaps for collective reasoning and speculation to occur. When a question or comment is brought to the group, children have an opportunity to think referentially. **Referential thinking** expands comprehension as children's own ideas are magnified through reference to others' points of view. Breaches are to be thought of not as a trail of errors made and corrected, but points in the text where understanding was deepened. The term breach is used, as opposed to the more common reference to *errors* or *miscues* in reading, to recognize that many of the reasons that groups stop during the reading process relate to a range of other factors besides the accuracy of word identification.

GLOSSARY BOX: REFERENTIAL THINKING

thinking about something in reference to another's point of view

In their classic book, *The New Circles of Learning*, David Johnson, Roger Johnson, and Edythe Holubec (1994) remind us of the power of cognitive conflict:

When managed constructively, controversy promotes uncertainty about the correctness of one's conclusions, an active search for more information, a reconceptualization of one's knowledge and conclusions, and, consequently, greater mastery and retention of the material being discussed and more frequent use of higher-level reasoning strategies. (p. 29)

Although the breaches that children are encouraged to air do not always amount to controversy per se, they nonetheless provoke disequilibrium and open the way for new learning.

Follow In: Responding to a Breach

The conversation following a breach is referred to as *follow in.* The term *follow in* was used by Jerome Bruner to describe the phenomenon of adult-child interaction whereby the adult *follows into* a child's focus of attention to help elaborate and extend understanding (Bruner, 1982). In such interactions, follow in promotes joint intersubjectivity and clarity of reference of what one is talking about. Within the context of Unison Reading, all points of discussion and resulting instructional points that occur after a breach are examples of *follow in.*

Conversations that follow into the breach are rich with learning potential, and it's important to know how to let the learning unfold. Rather than move in to provide answers or resolve questions, let the children lead. The primary impetus of Unison Reading is to support student agency and autonomy. So train yourself to hand over responsibility to the children to solve their own confusions. Ironically, in the wake of a breach, I've found the most powerful pedagogical response is to shrug your shoulders and gaze downward. This forces the children to take initiative to solve their own problems. Learning to ask questions that prompt kids to do their own thinking might mean you need to train yourself not to dominate. Try some of the prompts I've used in response to Unison Reading breaches, which are listed in Figure 1.3.

**GLOSSARY BOX:
METACOGNITIVE**

characterized by thinking about thinking

The Unison Reading experience provides two significant pathways for learning. First, it encourages **metacognitive** awareness during the reading process because children are held accountable for being attentive to their own thinking process. Second, breaching the group opens the possibility for understanding to be magnified by thinking about an idea in reference to the way that other group members think about the idea.

Mistakes, or "miscues" (Goodman, 1967) in the process of reading have long been considered important windows into the cognitive processes involved in reading. Metacognitive awareness develops to the extent that readers become aware of the thinking behind miscues. Unison Reading capitalizes on miscues as opportunities for group learning. Children are encouraged to become aware of their errors and points of confusion and use them as talking points in an ongoing dialog about the text at hand. Over time, interactive habits of mind are cultivated and with experience these become detachable skills that children learn to apply in the context of their independent reading.

When reading is defined as something that people do for socially purposeful reasons, accuracy of word reading is only one factor of concern. Equally important are interpersonal dynamics of the reading group and the function of the text, that influence how each member of the group participates and how the group functions. Traditional reading instruction practices encourage accurate reading performance and implicitly discourage "messing up." These traditions encourage children to view reading errors or miscues as mistakes that should be avoided. In Unison Reading groups, oral reading is not a performance of "who's the best," and errors are not "gotcha" opportunities for children to chide one another for "messing up." Comprehension of a text is a social

| Figure 1.3 | Examples of Teacher Responses to Breaches |

Group Process

"I heard us falter. Bring it back to the group when you hear us falter."

"Hold on, a couple of us stopped there. What just happened?"

"Can we make an observation here? I notice the three of us are talking a lot and you two are talking less and less. . . ."

"Do you agree or disagree?"

"Can you help her find a way?"

"That's interesting, you said . . . and you said . . . How are we going to figure out what it really says?"

"You breached the group. Good work. This is really important: Never miss a chance to make yourself smarter."

"Do you know what she's trying to say? No? Then ask her."

"Hold on, a couple of us stopped there. Let's talk about what's going on."

"You as a group need to decide where you want to stop and do some thinking work."

"Do we want to get back to the text?" (When discussion veers off course.)

Promotive Behaviors

"That was a good question, and it's a good thing you breached the group. But I could tell you were a little uncomfortable about stopping the group. Am I right? Listen guys. That's not ok. Everyone should feel safe enough to ask a question, and it's each of your responsibility to make sure your group mates feel comfortable. It's not ok for anyone to feel insecure about contributing to the group."

"When you disrupt the group it takes away the learning opportunities of others. You don't have the right to disrupt anyone's learning."

"You're doing a good job with promoting the group and looking out for others."

"Is everyone okay?"

"Act in a way that helps others in the group."

"I notice three of us are talking a lot, and you two are talking less and less. . . . What can we do about that?"

"You're saying a lot, Michael. Does anyone else have anything to say?"

Comprehension

"Do you want to figure out what *ordinance* means?"

"You used context clues to say that word. Tell us what you were thinking."

"How are we going to find out the meaning of that word?"

"When you bring your opinions to the group, you give yourself an opportunity to talk about what you think."

"Do you understand what that sentence says now?"

"Does anyone know what those are called?"

Fluency and Expression

"Can you read like you are reading a book on tape or narrating a nature program?"

"Hold on. There was a lot of information in that paragraph, and you read so fast. Do you need a little time to think about what you just read?"

GLOSSARY BOX: PROMOTIVE

characterized by promoting and supporting

GLOSSARY BOX: PRO-SOCIAL

characterized by supporting social cohesion and unity

---

accomplishment that materializes through an unfolding conversation as children pose and respond to their own questions *and* confusions.

When teachers are proactive in establishing **promotive** behaviors and involving group members in "facilitating each others' successes" (Johnson, Johnson, & Holubec, 1994, p. 29), **pro-social** behaviors become the group norm. Humility, compassion, empathy, and self-questioning are behaviors that are encouraged and supported by group members. These more receptive attitudes help create spaces for children to trust one another enough to collaborate in a social process of collective meaning making.

Triangulation

How does Unison Reading benefit all children? At the heart of literacy development is a capacity called *theory of mind* (ToM). Theory of mind is the innate human ability to understand that other people have mental states that are different from one's own, allowing us to predict what others might do, think, believe, or feel (Astington, Harris, & Olson, 1988). In the context of Unison Reading formats, ToM capacities allow children to revise their understanding of what they read by referencing others' perceptions about the text at hand. The process of socially referenced thinking is what is referred to in Unison Reading as *triangulation*. In the process of triangulation, children revise personal understandings about aspects of the text based on new data generated through group interactions. Through conversation and interaction with others, they have opportunities to deploy *theory of mind* capacities to assist in making sense of what they read. Cognitive scientists have termed the ability to monitor the behavior of others in dynamic social situations in order to organize thinking as "hot cognition" (as opposed to exercising "cold cognition," which is sufficient for static situations) (Stone, 2000; Tager-Flusberg & Sullivan, 2000). Through the process of triangulation, Unison Reading groups are rife with opportunities for children to exercise hot cognition. By emphasizing social processes on par with cognitive processes, Unison Reading enhances children's sociocognitive and socioperceptual skills and the manner in which children then apply these skills in interaction with others to read and comprehend texts.

As children accumulate experiences in triangulating their own ideas about a text against the ideas others in the group make of the text through triangulation, I believe they develop cognitive control. Why might this be so? First, children have the freedom to manage their involvement in dialogue about texts in which they have access to others' mental schemes. The process of exercising ToM to think about what others think engages the highest form of executive functioning (Goldberg, 2009). But these freedoms are tempered by the expectation to successfully participate in conventionalized communicative routines in which formerly learned skills are embedded. Jerome Bruner has suggested that it is the child's increasing capacity to take part in negotiated conventionalized ways of proceeding in everyday formats that contributes as a controlling factor in children's thought and behavior (1983). Successful participation in Unison Reading groups requires children to follow the rules and do their part to maintain group cohesion in pursuit of making sense of what they are reading. These opportunities support literacy development because they give children practice in gaining control over their thinking processes by calibrating their own ideas with those of others.

Introducing Unison Reading: An Example

In the following vignette I introduce Unison Reading to Jorell and Dewain, both sixth-grade delayed readers who scored a 2 on the state English language arts exam (on a scale of 4). They both speak dialects of American English (Jorell is Hispanic, of Dominican descent, and Dewain is African American). I begin with a question:

"Do you want me to show you something that will help you in your reading?" The boys nod their agreement, and I hand them a feature article from a local newspaper about Alex Rodriguez, a baseball player for the New York Yankees who had just been found to have previously used steroids. The text was chosen by their teacher who knew of their interest in baseball.

"What's this?" I ask, pointing to the text. They deliberate, and I tell them it's a sports article from the newspaper and briefly involve them in a discussion about the features of this genre of writing. The boys know something about Alex Rodriguez—that he's a baseball player and he plays for the Yankees—but they have only vague knowledge of the trouble he's recently faced. They both agree when I ask if they want to read it with me.

I say, "I'm going to show you a way to read today. It's called Unison Reading. Do you know what that word, unison, means?" They don't. I write the words unity, universe, united, and unison on paper. The boys and I discuss these words and their meanings, and I explain the meaning of the morpheme, "uni."

"This reading activity is designed to help you better understand what you read. It's not something you do all the time. But when you don't know a lot of words or concepts in the text, and when you want to partner with someone, it's a helpful way to read, and a lot more fun than reading on your own. Do you want to learn how?" They do.

So I explain, "The rules are simple. Everyone reads the same text out loud, and stays on the same word. You can't rush ahead, because then you leave your partner 'in the dust' and mess up his reading." I explain the meaning behind the phrase "in the dust," and make the connection that it's impossible to read with dust in your eyes. "The second rule is don't tolerate confusion! If you don't understand something or can't read a word, it's your responsibility to stop the group, let them know you're confused, and get them to help you solve your confusion. Each of you needs to be willing to stop the group when you either misread a word or don't understand something you've read. Do you think you have enough courage to stop the group when you don't understand something?" They say they do.

I draw a circle on a piece of paper with three dots spaced on the line of the circle equal distance from each other. "These," I say, pointing to the dots on the circle, "are each of us. We're each part of the same circle. This," I say, pointing to the center of the circle and coloring it in, "is what we read together. And when we read in Unison, this is what we make together," I say, pointing to the colored area in the middle. "It's our reading. The fun part about this way of reading is that when you come to something you don't know, you get to bring it into the center with your friends and get to figure it out," I say, pointing to the center of the circle.

"Normally when we read in school, we're made to think we should hide our mistakes and act as if we understand, even when we're confused. But in Unison Reading, you have a responsibility to the group to bring your mistakes and confusions to the center for discussion. That's what helps you become smarter and also helps the other kids in the group. That's also what makes Unison Reading fun. Your mistakes and confusions are opportunities for you to become smarter. Never miss out on an opportunity to make yourself smarter," I say somberly, alternately engaging each boy squarely in the eyes. "The only way for everyone to benefit from what each member of the group has to offer is to share the same reading experience. That's why it's important for everyone to read in sync. Reading in sync is kind of tricky, because you have to sort of listen to your friends while you read; you're looking out for them while you're reading. You want to give it a try?"

We spend about 20 minutes on two paragraphs of the story, discussing every feature that the boys hesitate about or that I anticipate they don't know. For their initial session, I assume responsibility to make sure unknown concepts or words are brought into the discussion. In other words, I do most of the interrupting this time around. But I end the first session with a group process observation, asking the boys, "Did you notice how I raised most of the questions?" They did. I continue, "Next time, you'll need to take more responsibility to raise your questions. Today I did the work for you. Next time you need to do most of the work on your own."

Because Unison Reading is significantly different from group reading formats students have previously experienced, it is important to explicitly explain the rules and processes so that the desired behaviors, dispositions, and attitudes are established with early exposure to the new experience. Unison Reading is based on the idea that competencies are an outcome of participation in certain practices. It is important that all children learn the "rules" so that they can hold themselves and one another accountable to them.

■ THE UNISON READING RECORD

Teachers record the reading process using the Unison Reading Record. (See Figure 1.4 for the first page of a sample Unison Reading Record and Appendix A for a complete Reading Record. You can also download a blank Reading Record at www.unisonreading.com.) This is done for several reasons:

- The process of noting breaches and responses helps the teacher build awareness of the ways in which children negotiate the challenges presented in texts and gain better insights into the complexities of group social interaction.
- The Record provides an instructional trail—evidence of points of instruction covered (as opposed to the traditional lesson plan, which outlines what the teacher determines should be taught). This documentation is useful for accountability purposes. Since the reading curriculum is not scripted or prescriptive according to pre-planned objectives, as is the case with conventional reading instruction approaches, but emerges organically through the process of children themselves raising instructional points, the Record provides a trail of learning points.
- Note taking forces the teacher to assume a reflective stance that enables more critical observation of the group process. Unlike conventional instructional formats, where teachers assume central authority in determining the course of instruction, Unison Reading requires teachers to follow up on the questions and comments students bring to their reading. Taking notes is a physical reminder that observation is of primary importance to teaching.
- The Record is a useful pedagogical tool. Children notice teachers in the act of recording, and discussions ensue that relate to the points documented. These conversations incorporate the metalanguage of reading and provide opportunities for metacognitive and metalinguistic awareness to develop.

The Unison Reading Record includes spaces for the title of the text, its genre form, and the date. The top of the record displays the four domains of reading: Social Processes, Genre, Comprehension, and Decoding and Strategic Processing. The domains are provided as reference points for observation and are used in coding the breaches.

The Domains: Categorizing What We Do As We Read

Social Processes and Genre are intentionally listed above Comprehension and Decoding/Strategic Processing on the Record to reinforce the fact that social purpose and context determine the nature of the reading process and the meanings derived. It's important to remember that these domains are merely ways to categorize the types of thinking we engage in as we read. In reality, we usually draw upon multiple domains simultaneously. The interconnectedness of each domain is represented by the arrows symbol. Each domain of reading is briefly described below:

- *Social Processes (SP)*. Unison Reading rests on the assumption that reading is a fundamentally social process, and that discrete reading skills and competencies are a direct consequence of the fundamental nature of the child's involvement as a social participant in reading situations. When a person possesses the social competencies that enable him or her to participate successfully in a particular social situation, the very act of participating generates new understanding. Breaches that fall under this domain have to do with Unison

Figure 1.4 Blank Unison Reading Record

Unison Reading Record

Title: _____ Genre Form: _____ Date: _____

SOCIAL PROCESSES (SP)

Unison Reading Rules	Coordinating Behaviors
Pacing—Fluency, Expression, and Prosody	Reading in Sync
Affective Factors (attitude/attention/engagement/motivation)	
Relational and Interpersonal Factors (resolving conflict/showing promotive behaviors)	

GENRE (G)

Text Form and Purpose	Genre Conventions
Syntax and Grammar	Punctuation
Layout, Text Features	Reader Stance (customs of reading text form)

COMPREHENSION (C)

Predict
Evaluate
Summarize
Infer, Draw Conclusions
Prior Knowledge

Question
Synthesize
Create Images
Vocabulary
Interpretation (Fluency/Expression/Punctuation)

DECODING AND STRATEGIC PROCESSING (D)

Strategy Use (rereading/looking back, self-monitoring, self-correcting, cros checking, reading ahead, punctuation)
Phonics (blending and segmenting, letter-sound correspondence, word families, grapheme/phoneme relationships, onset/rime)
Word Reading Strategies (contextual analysis; morphological relationships; relating known words to unknown words)

Record **BREACHES** in order of occurrence

CODE/ Breach	Teacher	Student 1	Student 2	Student 3	Student 4	Student 5	Record INSTRUCTIONAL POINT that follows in to corresponding breach or insight
#1							
#2							
#3							
#4							

Reading as a basic social practice and the ways in which each participant contributes to the whole of the group experience. Issues coded "SP" include attention to basic Unison Reading rules such as reading audibly and staying in sync ("I can't hear Omar."); engagement and attitudes ("Demetrius, you aren't paying attention!"); interpersonal conflicts or promotive behaviors ("Steven is kicking me under the table," or, "Mei Yi, I haven't heard you say anything for the last few minutes. Is everything ok?"); and pacing, fluency, or prosody ("Y'all didn't pause at the comma. Y'all have to stop at the comma so it sounds right.").

• *Genre (G)*. Breaches that fall under this domain have to do with the basic purpose of the text being read and the conventions typically followed when reading this type of text. The ways in which texts in each genre are structured—their features and layout, language style, and use of line, space, and image—relate to their respective purposes. And readers participate in particular social conventions when reading these various text types, resulting in reading experiences that are characterized by the reciprocal relationship between readers' intentions and text purpose. For example, expository texts usually incorporate a number of features such as subtitles, captions, diagrams, illustrations and photographs, each of which are read in a sequence determined by the reader's intentions. As children read across a range of genres, they have opportunities to synchronize their actions and intentions with the purpose of the text at hand.

• *Comprehension (C)*. Breaches in this domain have to do with the kinds of meanings children make given the situation in which the text is being read, the kind of text being read, and the intentions of the person(s) reading. These are examples of comprehension breaches: At a tense point in a feature article about a diver who lost consciousness, Min asks, "I wonder what will happen next?" Or eighth-grade Dominique comments, "That's just wrong," in response to a feature article about a proposal to pass a city ordinance banning baggy jeans. A group of eighth-grade boys read, "He had to 'pur-fikt' his game" instead of the intended, "he had to 'per-fekt' his game," a comprehension-vocabulary breach.

• *Decoding/Strategic Processing (D)*. Breaches that fall in this domain have to do with the technical qualities of written language. For example, when a first grader breached her Unison Reading group when one of her peers read, "Dabby went to the store," instead of "Daddy went to the store," and she explained, "It's not Dabby because those are d's, not b's," the breach was coded "D." Or when a group of sixth graders, including advanced and delayed readers, read a caption in which the word *season* was hyphenated, they all initially read two words: *sea* and *son*. Someone breached the group because the sentence didn't make sense. After some discussion, the confusion was resolved (as it happens, by one of the less advanced readers in the group).

Recording the Group Reading Experience

On the Unison Reading Record, under the description of the domains, are spaces to enter the names of each participant in the reading group. The teacher's name is recorded first, followed by the names of each of the children in the group.

When the group's reading is breached, the teacher records comments and behaviors. Every breach is recorded on a new line and coded by domain. As children stop the group to raise questions or give comments, the substance of their comments are recorded in their respective columns. Turns in conversation that ensue after a breach are numbered in the order they occur in children's respective columns. The comments of the child who breaches the group are numbered "1." The child who next responds is number "2," and so on. The space is left blank for children who don't participate in the follow-in conversations.

As a member of the group, the teacher is entitled to breach the reading process, but should do so only if he or she feels it is a point that *must* be made. As previously pointed out, it is important not to dominate, as the overarching intent of Unison Reading is to provide support for children to take responsibility and initiative in the reading process. Sometimes, when I'm working with a group new to Unison Reading, I invariably make the majority of breaches. But then I point out the students' responsibility for stopping the group in future sessions.

Conversations naturally center on the point of focus/confusion, and the substance of this conversation becomes the *instructional point*, which is recorded in the far-right column on the line of the corresponding breach. The factors listed at the top of the record within each of the domains of reading are references for instructional points. As conversation takes place after a breach, you should try to identify which reading domain is most relevant and use the list of factors to help clarify the issues being raised. The list of factors within each domain can serve as a "cheat sheet" you can reference in your note taking to help you become more conscious of the range of cognitive and social processes children are using as they read.

Conversation sometimes unfolds around a point that can be clarified by notes taken on the Unison Reading Record. At these times, it's sometimes useful to stop the group and share notes about what children said to help them work through an idea. At the end of the session, share collective achievements with the group. You might briefly review the instructional points raised in order to remind them how much they learned.

Using Process Checks to Monitor the Session

The group process supports collective understanding of a text, so group processes are taught as explicitly as cognitive processes through *process checks.* When children are still learning the rules of Unison Reading and how to function in the group, I stop at various points during the Unison Reading session to do a process check. Children know it is an expectation that they participate and offer insights to the group. But some have to *learn* how to participate, especially if they are accustomed to teacher-dominated instructional groups. This is where the process check is necessary.

A process check is simply a teacher-initiated breach in which feedback is shared about the group process. Typically teachers share notes from the Unison Reading Record, pointing out things like, "Look how many times I breached the group! It's important for you to take some of that responsibility." Or, "Look at the record and notice whether or how much you are participating. If you aren't participating enough, are you letting someone else do all the work?" Or, "Are you dominating the conversation without letting others have a chance to say things?"

Process checks serve as a feedback loop for each child to gain insight about their social contributions and a tool for helping them to develop social competencies needed in groups. Over time, children begin to see patterns in their own behaviors and those of other children, and they learn to use the language of instruction to describe these behaviors.

The Unison Reading Record provides a trail of group learning. With the record in hand, it is possible to analyze and make judgments about the benefits and limitations of the learning experience—insights that can inform future instruction in powerful ways.

Examples of Unison Reading Records

In this section I present content from sample Unison Reading Records from three classrooms—Tara Clark's first-grade classroom, Lauren Casion's fifth-grade classroom, and Emily Jarrell's eighth-grade classroom—to illustrate the note-taking conventions and developmental behaviors that come to light through Unison Reading assessment. The Unison Reading Analysis form, used here to analyze the three sample reading sessions, isn't necessary to complete for every session (in fact, analyzing every record would be a poor use of time). But occasionally it is helpful to formally analyze Unison Reading Records in order to detect patterns of participation and instructional content. The Unison Reading Analysis form is also available at unisonreading.com. Guidelines for analyzing the Records are included at the end of this section.

From Tara Clark's First-Grade Classroom

The first record features Eddie, an English language learner; Maria, a fluent English speaker whose home language is Spanish; and Michael, also an English language learner. The children had chosen to read the advice column from *Highlights* magazine for this week's Unison Reading group. Content from the Record is featured in Figure 1.5 and the Unison Reading Analysis in Figure 1.6.

Figure 1.5 Sample Content From Completed Unison Reading Record, Tara Clark, First Grade

Title: <u>Dear *Highlights*: My Friend Says She Will Keep a Secret</u>   Genre Form: <u>Advice column</u>   Date: <u>2/2/2010</u>

Record **BREACHES** in order of occurrence

CODE/ Breach	Teacher Clark	Student 1 Eddie (ESL)	Student 2 Maria	Student 3 Michael (ESL)	Student 4	Student 5	Record INSTRUCTIONAL POINT that follows in to corresponding breach or insight
#1 D	(3) It looks like that's how you would say it, but it's actually *says /ses/.*	(1) We said *said.* It doesn't look like *said.* (says)	(2) Says /sas/ (with a long a sound)	X			• Decoding (said for says)
#2 D	(4) When someone figures out a word you can't just copy them. You need to ask them. "How did you figure that out?"	(3) Secret	(1) Secret (6) Se-cret (Using fingers to show the parts of the word)	(2) Secret (5) How did you know that Maria?			• Decoding—chunking • Social Processing— personal responsibility
#3 G		(1) This looks like a question. (3) This means it is a question.	X	(2) Yeah, it has a question mark, Eddie. (4) Yeah.			• Punctuation conventions— question mark
#4 D	(6) Is it enjoy or enjoying?	(2) No, this is not ever. (4) enjoying (8) I don't agree.	(1) Ever (10) 'ing'	(3) Can we stretch it out? (5) What's enjoying Eddie? The end doesn't have 'ing.' (7) Enjoy (9) It don't have . . . (11) 'ing.' It don't have 'ing.'			• Decoding • Word endings (ing)
#5 SP		X	X	(1) Stop! Eddie's reading too fast.			• Pacing

14

Turn						Focus/Skills
#6 SP		(1) Let's go back to 'if.' (3) It has a capital.	(2) Do we really have to go back to 'if'?	X		• Tracking/coordinating reading
#7 D	(4) Might means maybe	(2) It's not 'must.' I see silent 'gh.' Might. Might. What does this mean?	(1) Must (3) I might go with my friend.	X		• Decoding/phonics
#8 D	(3) Michael, don't copy Eddie. You need to stop the group.	(1) Best (5) "B" says /b/. E says /e/. St says /st/.	X	(2) Best (4) How did you know that Eddie?		• Phonics • Importance of breaching
#9 D		(1) Past (4) Pa says /pa/. St says /st/.	(2) How did you know that Eddie?	(3) How did you know that Eddie?		• Phonics
#10 D	(3) They're trying to figure it out. Tell him. (7) Does it sound like a word you know?	(1) We are stuck here. It's a long word. (4) We're trying to figure it out. R-e-m. (6) Remember. (10) It means you don't forget.	(5) Ok. R-e-m. I got it. (8) Re-mem-ber.	(2) Can we go back. I'm not there. (9) Remember means you know it.		• Decoding (phonics) • Vocabulary (remember)
#11 SP		(1) Mistake (4) Hey, you say it after me. (7) Because I think everyone makes a mistake in the classroom.	(2) Mistake (5) Stop. I forgot what to say.	(3) Where Eddie? (6) How do you know that?		• Rules
#12 D	(2) What can we do? (13) Private means secret (diction-ary)	(1) Pppp (5) Pr is a blend, not a chunk. (7) How did you know that Maria? (10) Can you say more about that? (12) Ms. Clark, can you help?	(1)Pppp (4) I think we should look for chunks. (6) Private! (8) Private means we have to be alone to do something. (11) I don't know.	(1)Pppp (3) Let's stretch it out. (9) Huh? (14) My friend tells me the same thing he say don't tell anybody.		• Decoding (blends) • Sight-word vocabulary • Vocabulary (word meanings) • Dictionary

Figure 1.6   Unison Reading Record Analysis, Tara Clark, First Grade

Unison Reading Analysis

Total breaches	12
Social Processes	3 33%
Genre	1 8%
Comprehension	0 0%
Decoding	8 67%

Members	% Participated	% Breached
Eddie (Group Leader)	92%	62%
Maria	67%	23%
Michael	75%	15%
Clark	58%	0%

Instructional Inventory

Social Processes	Genre	Comprehension	Decoding
• Pacing • Tracking • Coordinating reading • Importance of breaching	• Punctuation conventions	• Dictionary definition (private)	• Sight word (said) • Chunking • Word endings (ing) • Decoding/phonics (might) • Phonics (best) • Phonics (past) • Phonics (remember) • Blends • Sight word/vocabulary • Vocabulary—word meanings (private)

Notice how the children take the lead in posing questions and addressing one another's confusions when they can't decode words or their group process is out of sync. This conversational independence is a result of Tara's conscious effort to give children agency in facilitating groups. Notice Tara never breaches the group. Her participation is limited to following into children's confusions. When they are able to resolve their own confusions, she gives them autonomy to do so. Her participation is limited to the tail end of conversational turns in only about 50% of the breaches when her intervention is necessary to address confusions the children themselves are unable to resolve.

Also notice the inventory of instructional points that arise in the session. Most of the time the children turn their attention to social process and decoding issues. From a developmental standpoint, this makes sense. When they put their heads together around a text, kindergarten and first-grade children are faced with the challenge of working out the technicalities of a new and unfamiliar written symbol system. Naturally, they devote attention to solving the mysteries of how it works. Young children are also just getting comfortable working in social groups beyond the safety and comfort of their home environments. Turn taking, listening, and taking another's perspective are all skills that have to be learned. The Records of children in primary grades should be rich with Social Process breaches because children are learning how to use dialog to learn. Notice how Tara supports this learning. Specifically, Tara's participation on examples #2 and #8 prompted Michael to take initiative for resolving his confusions by asking questions or stopping the group when he had a question.

Tara commented about the Unison Reading session:

This Unison Reading Record is of a group of three first graders—two boys and a girl. The group is reading an advice column from a *Highlights Magazine* entitled, "My Friend Says She Will Keep My Secret." The three diverse learners in this group created an interesting dynamic. And Unison Reading created opportunities for each of them to exercise strengths, practice needed skills and strategies, and discuss their thinking. They've come to this session already invested, interested, and intrigued, having signed-up for this text based on interest and challenge level.

Eddie and Michael are English Language learners who speak Chinese at home. The other group member, Maria, is a fluent English speaker. Eddie and Michael differ in terms of their approach to problem solving, decoding, articulating thoughts, and supporting the group processes. Maria is very social and does not seek out these boys outside of Unison Reading. Interestingly, they sign up for the same text, all three interested in the ideas around keeping secrets.

Eddie breaches the group often. He breaches when he makes a mistake, when he hears others make mistakes, when he's confused, or when he has something to say to support the group work. He never hesitates and is a very active participant who is concerned with establishing mutual understanding within the group. Unison Reading gives Eddie a space where he can practice articulating his thoughts in a way others can understand. This is a challenging task for an English Language Learner like Eddie. He often is so excited when he's speaking that it becomes difficult to understand what he is saying. Participating in Unison Reading, Eddie is held accountable to the pace in which he speaks and the extent to which he is understood by others. It's important to Eddie to be understood, and he knows now that when he speaks to the group, the rate of his speech will affect the extent to which he is understood. He views his contribution as valuable and sees the importance of being promotive of other's learning. Eddie has grown in that he now monitors the rate of his speech and the words he chooses to use to explain his thinking clearly.

Michael is also an English language learner but presents with a very different set of challenges and approach. Michael doesn't breach the group often and opportunities to learn pass him by. This is evident in the Unison Reading Record when Michael repeats what other group members say without understanding how to decode and say the word himself. Earlier in the school year, Michael would not stop the group when necessary. He repeated words that other children figured out, or mumbled something that sounded like the word, pretending to read it. The group members and I remind Michael not to copy but to stop the group so that the group can explain how they solved the unknown word. Michael is progressing. Being a member in a Unison Reading group and adhering to the rules helps hold Michael accountable for taking responsibility to resolve his confusions. Michael shows signs of progress when he breaches the group and asks, "How did you know that word?" Not only is Michael learning what to do when he doesn't know a word, he's learning to be metacognitive of himself as a reader. He's learning to articulate his confusions, seize the moment, and see opportunities to breach the group as learning opportunities arise. Finally for him, breaches are becoming mechanisms he uses to help himself grow, learn, and feel more competent in what he knows and can do. Unison Reading supports him as he grows an awareness of the process of learning to read. It's a huge step for this first grader!

(Continued)

(Continued)

Maria is socially competent and can contribute significantly to discussions but she often gets sidetracked as she talks. She goes off on tangents that cause her to forget her talking points. Her comments are often unrelated to the conversation and she struggles to follow in to the thinking of others. Maria also has a history of not initiating problem solving independently. It is evident in the Unison Reading Record how Maria is practicing the very skills that she needs to hone. She follows in and supports the group in figuring out the words *secret* and *enjoy*, and even demonstrates her strategy when asked to explain how she figured out the word. She also is the first one to breach the group in an attempt to solve the word *enjoy* and says "ever." Unison Reading creates the very opportunities Maria needs in order to strengthen her ability to contribute and respond appropriately in a discussion, follow into the thinking of others, and take an active stance toward problem solving.

Participating in this group was entirely promotive to the learning each individual needs. Unison Reading creates space and opportunities for diverse learners to come together with joint intentions and support each other as they navigate the text; practicing and articulating what they already know, what they need to know, and learning from the insights of others. Reading this text created quite a stir for these first graders. Reading about the seriousness of secrets and trusting someone with a secret challenged their understanding. As first graders, prior to reading this column, they did not consider secrets to be serious. They did not consider the ins and outs of trusting someone with a secret. This text stretched their understanding. Once the group finished reading there was a sense of a healthy disequilibrium created by the ideas this text presented. The ideas in the text didn't match up with what they thought they knew about secrets. It's quite possible that for the first time they were considering a different perspective of telling and keeping secrets or learned about the concept of secrets for the first time.

From Lauren Casion's Fifth-Grade Classroom

The second sample Record features Janet, an English language learner; Ming, also an English language learner; Becky, a fluent English speaker from a home where Chinese is spoken; Janelle, a low-performing reader, fluent in English, from a home where Spanish is the dominant language; and Justin, a low-performing reader, who like Janelle is a fluent English speaker from a Spanish language background. This record was taken during the extended day supplemental instructional program where Unison Reading is used as the reading intervention program. This group of students read Cynthia Rylant's *Slower Than the Rest* over the course of two days. Though teachers complete a new Unison Reading Record each time a group meets, I collapsed content taken on Records from both days into Figure 1.7.

Lauren's Record shows that she is a keen observer and listener. She captures detailed information about each child's contribution to the reading dialog and summarizes instructional points that emerge from the conversation. This record shows evidence of extensive autonomy on the part of the children to manage and resolve their confusions. You can follow the chain of conversation initiated by each breach to explore how their dialog supported extensive comprehension and word work. Interestingly, in this particular record there are no Social Process breaches, an example of how, as children become comfortable with the Unison Reading protocol and as they acquire greater social competence with age they are better able to manage conversational convention. When groups naturally function smoothly, children are able to navigate meaning with relative independence.

The children's independence is not surprising in light of Lauren's skill. Like Tara, Lauren allows students take the lead in shaping the dialog and only follows into the conversation with comments to clarify confusions that can't be resolved by the children themselves. Also like Tara above, Lauren never breaches the group; she participates in only four conversations to intervene when the children are unable to resolve confusion, allowing children maximum responsibility.

Figure 1.7 Sample Content From Completed Unison Reading Record, Lauren Casion, Fifth Grade

Title: Slower than the Rest (Every Living Thing)   Genre Form: Narrative   Date: 2/3/2010

Record **BREACHES** in order of occurrence

CODE/ Breach	Teacher Casion	Student 1 Janet (ESL)	Student 2 Ming (ESL)	Student 3 Becky	Student 4 Janelle	Student 5 Justin	Record INSTRUCTIONAL POINT that follows in to corresponding breach or insight
#1 C	(7) This is from the same book as "Papa's Parrot"	(4) I think the turtle is going to be slower than someone (6) Maybe a character will change.	(5) There will probably be a problem and a solution	(2) Turtles	(1) Let's think what this could be about . . . (3) Maybe the main character is a turtle	X	• Approaching a text • Making predictions • Connecting what you know from similar stories
#2 C		(2) It means he saw it first (4) And he's a boy (6) I agree . . . (Demonstrates) (8) The driver must have stopped the car too (11) I agree with Ming	(1) What does the author mean "Leo was the first one to spot the turtle?" (7) I agree . . . they stopped and looked (10) We can infer it's outside	X	(3) So now we know Leo is the main character (5) I think "jerked" means their heads turned in a certain way (9) Is the turtle outside the car or inside the car?	X	• Asking questions • Making inferences • Envisioning • Vocabulary ("Spot")
#3 D	(2) How can we figure it out? (7) Wait—what does the first part of the sentence show us?	(5) I think it means his mom is "interested" in turtles (9) And he doesn't care about the turtle	(4) I think we should read on now that we know how to say it (6) I think it makes sense if you plug it in (8) His dad wants to cook the turtle (11) I think we should revise some of our predictions	(1) Stop! I don't know this word.	(10) Oh! So Leo's mom cares about turtles	(3) Chunk it . . . It's sym-pa-thet-ic	• Chunking • Vocabulary ("Sympathize") • Using context clues

(Continued)

Figure 1.7 (Continued)

Day II #4 D	(5) So what do we do?	(2) [Attempts chunking the rest] (7) And it makes sense if you substitute it	(1) Stop! What's this word? We know the first part: 'con' like 'construction paper' (6) Read on. So Janelle is right because we know Charlie is friendly	(3) But what does it mean? (8) [Does a dictionary check]	(4) Maybe he's being nice? (9) [Adds to "personal word book"]	X · Chunking · Long/short vowel sounds · Vocabulary ("Congenial") · Using context clues
#5 D	(4) What part of speech? What action is being modified? (6) So how is he swimming?	(2) Maybe it means "swimming deep" Wait, that doesn't make sense (7) Scared, fast	(8) [Connects personal experience with pet turtle moving the same way]	(1) What does "frantically" mean? (5) Adverb Swimming (10) Dictionary check	(3) Maybe it's the *way* he swims	X · Vocabulary ("Frantically") · Parts of speech · Context clues · Base word
#6 C		(2) I'm confused. I thought Leo was in fourth grade (4) [Rereads to clarify] (6) It means like smart	(1) So Leo is treating Charlie like a real friend because every day he talks to him (8) I disagree . . . . I think the problem might be he gets teased by other kids at school	(3) Well, we know he's 10 years old (5) I don't understand "wise like old people"	(7) I can make a prediction—I think Leo might be into trouble (9) Now I think Leo brought Charlie to help him with his assignment	X · Drawing conclusions · Making inferences · Predicting · Rereading

Figure 1.8 Lauren's Chart, September–June

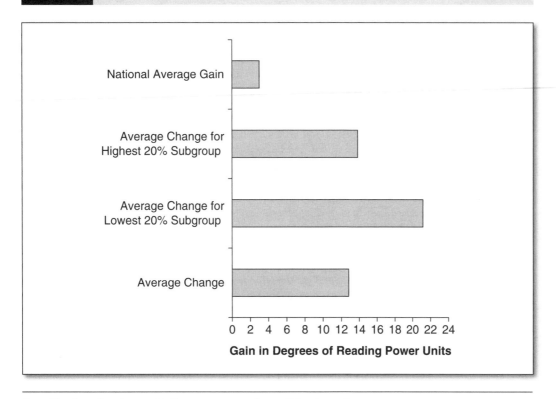

Note: Number of students = 21. Scores are reported on a 100-point scale.

Students in Lauren's class appear to benefit from these opportunities to practice independence as readers, judging by their standardized test results. We use the Degrees of Reading Power assessment as the school-wide benchmarking system in Grades 2–8; the assessment reports progress in "DRP" units. After one year of the Unison Reading program in Lauren's classroom, her students (N = 21) made average gains in reading of 12.7 DRP units, over four times the national average of 3 DRP units per year for eighth grade (Questar Assessment, 2000). Students who initially scored in the lowest 20% on the DRP in the fall gained an average of 21 DRP units over the course of the year; and students who scored in the highest 20% in the fall gained an average of 13.8 DRP units over the course of the year. Lauren offers an account of the group's process detailed through her observation on the Unison Reading Record:

This Unison Reading Record is from a group who gets supplemental instruction after school, about a third of my class participate in this program. Two students in the group are ESL and three are low-performing readers. The text was *Slower Than the Rest,* by Cynthia Rylant (1985). It was a challenging text. I think that personally at this point in the school year I'm seeing a lot of growth in terms of the conversations they have. For example, the types of confusions they're raising have evolved. In the beginning of the year they might have stopped the group to say "you said learn for learned." Now they're stopping the group for more meaningful reasons. For example, Ming, who is an ESL student, stopped the group and said, "What does the author mean? *Leo was the first to* spot *the turtle."* He didn't know what that meant, that phrase . . . to *spot* something. And so then the whole group comes in and supports him. Like Becky comes in and says, it means

(Continued)

> (Continued)
>
> he saw it first. . . . Then there was confusion about the word *jerked*. Because in the story, everyone in the car jerked their heads to see the turtle. So then Janet said, "I think it means their heads turned in a certain way." Then she demonstrates for the group what that means, to jerk your head.
>
> They're stopping for vocabulary words they don't know, and they're coming up with strategies for how to solve their problem. So they got stuck on the word *sympathetic,* and Justin suggested chunking it. Then once they figured out how to chunk the word and say the word, they come in with all these different ways to think about what that word means. Ming suggested reading on, and then after the group had read on, Janet said, "I think it means the mom is very interested in turtles. And the mother is sympathetic to the turtle. She doesn't want to run the turtle over." And then Ming suggested to substitute the word interested to see if it makes sense. Then I had to come in and teach, in this sentence, the first part of the sentence the father was muttering something about turtle soup. And the mother was sympathetic. And so I had to come in and say we had to pay attention to the first part of the sentence. And that's a direct connection to the second part of the sentence, and that's what's giving us a clue to what the word *sympathetic* means. After we figured out what it meant, after this sort of flow, they said they needed to revise some of their thinking. Because in the beginning they had made all these predictions about what the story was going to be about. And at this point they realized that their prediction was wrong, and they had to change their idea.

An analysis of Lauren's Unison Reading Record appears in Figure 1.9. The group met over the course of two days. Ming, an English language learner, is participating and following into each breach. He breached the group one time. Janet, another English language learner, never breached the group, but she participated 100% of the time. Such high levels of engagement and participation are good signs for English language learners, who are only able to learn to master the language by using it. Justin, however, participates infrequently, and this might become a source of concern. On the first day he only participated in 25% of the conversations, and he was absent the second day. Moreover, he never breached the group. Learning results from participation, and the child who doesn't participate or who is frequently absent will lack sufficient learning opportunities. The Record is a good way to keep track of patterns of participation in children who are reserved, reluctant, or disengaged.

Another interesting point in Lauren's Record Analysis is the issue of instructional focus. For decades, the field of reading has engaged in a circular debate about the relative merits of skills versus meaning instruction. Interestingly, when we allow children to take responsibility for managing their own learning, and they do so in response to the exigencies of the situation, they invariably balance attention to skills and meaning. In this particular group, the children attended mostly to meaning making at the passage level (compared to their primary school mates from Tara's classroom, who focused primarily on Social Process and Decoding). But within the context of making meaning, they deployed phonics knowledge, knowledge of grammar and syntax, decoding strategies, and logic related to the use of reading strategies. Also interesting, when this fifth-grade Record is compared to the Record from Tara Clark's first-grade students, we see much less emphasis on social processing issues and decoding. Naturally, fifth graders have more expertise with both working in groups and working with letter-sound relationships. First graders, more novice users of the written English system, allocate more attention to synchronizing their cooperative behaviors and mastering the technical features of texts.

From Emily Jarrell's Eighth-Grade Classroom

In the Unison Reading Record of these eighth graders' reading of a music review, the potential of dialogic learning in adolescence comes to life (See Unison Reading Record, Figure 1.10). As you will read in Chapter 2, the grouping practices of Unison Reading force children to organize themselves into diverse groups. The group featured in Emily's Record

Figure 1.9	Unison Reading Record Analysis, Lauren Casion, Fifth Grade

Unison Reading Analysis

Total breaches	6
Social Processes	0 0%
Genre	0 0%
Comprehension	3 50%
Decoding	3 50%

Members	% Participated	% Breached
Janet (Group Leader)	100%	0%
Ming	100%	50%
Becky	83%	33%
Janelle	100%	17%
Justin (absent second day)	17%	0%
Casion	67%	0%

Instructional Inventory

Social Processes	Genre	Comprehension	Decoding
		<ul><li>Approaching a text</li><li>Making predictions</li><li>Connecting what you know from similar stories</li><li>Asking questions</li><li>Making inferences</li><li>Envisioning</li><li>Vocabulary (frantic)</li><li>Parts of speech</li><li>Context clues</li><li>Base word</li><li>Drawing conclusions</li><li>Making inferences</li><li>Predicting</li><li>Rereading</li></ul>	<ul><li>Chunking</li><li>Vocabulary (sympathetic)</li><li>Using context clues</li><li>Long/short vowel sounds</li><li>Vocabulary (congenial)</li></ul>

Figure 1.10 Sample Content From Completed Unison Reading Record, Emily Jarrell, Eighth Grade

Title: New Jay-Z Strengthens Hip-Hop's Foundation   Genre Form: Music Review   Date: 2/12/10

Record **BREACHES** in order of occurrence

CODE/ Breach	Teacher Emily	Student 1 Joseph	Student 2 Ella	Student 3 Mariel	Student 4 Edgar	Student 5 Jeremy	Record INSTRUCTIONAL POINT that follows in to corresponding breach or insight
#1 G		(2) Weird?	X	1) Why updated and published on the same day?	X	X	• Conventions of dating internet sources
#2 C		(1) He was retiring? It says post retirement.	X	X	X	X	• Prior knowledge (is Jay-Z retired?) • Vocabulary—*post* meaning after
#3 C		2) I'm better than everyone.	X	(1) What's 'cocky'?	(3) You brag about yourself.	X	• Vocabulary (cocky)
#4 C		(2) How is it possible that you can be humble and cocky?	(1) What is humble?	(3) Maybe he's like that with his wife.	X	ARRIVES LATE (4) He is not about all the things most people sing about.	• Comprehension (personality traits) • Vocabulary (cocky and humble) • Prior knowledge (challenging stereotypes)
#5 C	(3) De-meaning. Prefix/suffix. Demeaning. A lot of hip-hop is demeaning toward women.	(2) What's demeaning? (5) Back to the article lyrics . . . the lyrics are demeaning. (8) Do you know what that means?	(9) Not really.	(1) That's kind of demeaning. Lyrics: *"I'm from the apple, which means I'm the MAC. She's a PC, she lives in my lap."* (6) What? (10) It's gross.		(4) But a lot of women in hip hop are respected. (7) Oh, no, no, those are totally demeaning. I'm not gonna say it. (9) It's demeaning.	• Comprehension (evaluation—"that's kind of demeaning") • Vocabulary (demeaning)

Figure 1.11 Emily's Chart, September–June

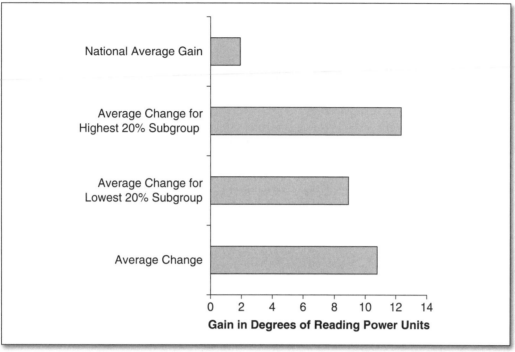

Note: Number of students = 108. Scores are reported on a 100-point scale.

is a case in point. Mariel and Ella are two White girls from middle-class households who joined Jeremy, Joseph, and Edgar, three Hispanic/Latino boys from low-income households. According to the reading benchmarking assessment, Mariel is one of the highest-performing readers in the class, and Jeremy is one of the two lowest. Three of the children in the group receive Special Education Teacher Support Services (SETSS).

In this session, the group is reading a review of a rap by Jay-Z. At one point, Mariel suggested that the lyrics were *demeaning*. At that point there was confusion about the meaning of the word *demeaning*, and a conversation ensued. This led to a discussion about the tendency within the genre of hip hop for women to be portrayed in demeaning ways. Jeremy then responded that a lot of women in hip hop are respected. Prompted by this dissonance, the kids turned back to the text to analyze Jay-Z's lyrics against the criteria of demeaning, eventually concluding about the lyrics, "it's demeaning," and "it's gross."

Emily commented about this group:

> The routines of Unison Reading force them to be a part of one of the groups that are up for the week. For this particular group, kids came together around a topic that would never have happened without the structure—these two middle-class White girls with Joseph and Jeremy, kids from the neighborhood [housing projects]. And they were all working together very promotively.
>
> The fact that these five kids worked together would have never happened in any leveled or guided reading grouping. Not only does this group consist of kids of mixed reading levels, but they are also showing a willingness to take risks in the texts they choose.
>
> Mariel and Ella chose a text that was outside their comfort level in terms of topics and kids who would probably sign up for the group. Mariel was sort of the leader here. She came to this group and sort of brought Ella in. She comes with full energy. And what was nice, it allowed an opportunity for Jeremy to be a teacher. He was the one who had the background knowledge on the topic.

Unison Reading groups constantly change, and the children learn to use the groups not only to explore new topics through texts, but also to practice their identities and explore their senses of themselves. And Emily's students, like Lauren's, demonstrated impressive gains in reading achievement as measured by the DRP assessment. After one year of the Unison Reading program in Emily's classroom, the eighth graders in the Jacob Riis School gained an average of 11.0 DRP units, over five times the national average of 2 DRP units per year for eighth grade (Questar Assessment, 2000). Students who initially scored in the lowest 20% on the DRP in September gained an average of 9.1 DRP units over the course of the year, and students who scored in the highest 20% on the DRP gained an

Figure 1.12	Unison Reading Record Analysis, Emily Jarrell, Eighth Grade

Unison Reading Analysis

Total breaches	4
Social Processes	0 0%
Genre	1 25%
Comprehension	3 75%
Decoding	8 67%

Members	% Participated	% Breached
Joseph (group leader)	100%	25%
Ella	25%	25%
Mariel	75%	50%
Edgar	25%	25%
Jeremy	25%	0%
Emily	0%	0%

Instructional Inventory

Social Processes	Genre	Comprehension	Decoding
	• Dating conventions for internet sources • Hip hop's treatment of women	• Prior knowledge • Vocabulary (cocky) • Vocabulary (humble) • Personality traits (cocky yet humble?) • Prior knowledge • Critical reading of lyrics against criteria of meaning of "demeaning."	

average of 12.6 DRP units over the course of the year. Eighth-grade English language learners who were integrated into the general education classroom where they participated in Unison Reading groups with their English-speaking peers gained an average of 9.0 DRP units over the course of the year, tripling the average rate of growth of 3 DRP units reported for ELLs nationally (Maculaitis, 2001). Children in the eighth-grade self-contained special education classroom who, in addition to the program specified in their IEPs, took part in Unison Reading in the general education program gained an average of 12.2 DRP units over the course of the year. Overall growth in reading achievement among all children in the eighth grade was dramatic (see Chapter 5 for a full description of school-wide assessment results).

Analyzing the Unison Reading Record

You've seen examples of the Unison Reading Analysis as completed by three different teachers (in Figures 1.5, 1.7, and 1.10). What follows is a description of the process these teachers used to analyze the Unison Reading Record of classroom sessions and to note their summaries on the Analysis form, along with the rationale for tracking this kind of information. (Find blank Unison Reading Record Analysis Form in Appendix A.) Essentially, the periodic summarizing of this information serves as a tool to monitor the patterns and effectiveness of students' learning over time, and allows teachers to adjust their instruction accordingly.

1. *Analyze breaches.* Scan the coding in the far-left column of the record, tallying the number of breaches initiated under each domain of reading (social processes, genre, comprehension, and decoding/strategic processing). Divide the number of breaches in each category by the total breaches to arrive at the average number of times the group breached the process for each domain.

Why?
Doing this will allow you to monitor patterns over time. Once children master the social processes of group reading and assume personal responsibility for participating, they more readily attend to text features and meanings. As children resolve social process issues, and they become less a focus of attention and learning, children begin to breach the group for other reasons. As groups begin to function with relative independence and distributed responsibility, children pose questions and make comments across the other domains as they critically analyze ideas, technical features of texts, and genre considerations.

2. *Determine who breaches and how much.* Tally the number of times each group member breached the group. Divide each member's number of breaches by the total number of breaches.

Why?
It is important to look for balanced participation over time. Initially, you, as teacher, will breach the group most often as you teach into social process concerns and encourage children to take responsibility for their own thinking. Over time, children will assume responsibility to participate equally. Some children, however, take longer to take initiative. For example, children who are highly timid or shy, or English language learners who, in addition to learning the language are also learning the communicative conventions of English, will take longer to become comfortable in breaching the group. You will want to monitor their involvement and look for gains over time in the average number of times they breach the group.

3. *Keep track of inventory teaching points.* Scan the far-right column of the Record from the first line to the last. On a separate page, list the specific factors under each domain that

the group attended (for example, *reading in sync* would be a factor under the domain Social Processes). As you inventory the instructional points, write specific points of instruction beneath the heading for each factor.

Why?
This exercise will help hone your awareness of the way in which instructional opportunities arise in the group. Again, as children assume more responsibility and their groups run more independently, the quality of instruction improves.

CHILDREN'S SELF-RESPONSIBILITY AND ACCOUNTABILITY

Unison Reading is based on a self-responsibility theory of learning in which children are held accountable to participate in academic situations in personally and socially constructive ways (Olson, 2003, 2007). Rather than teachers telling children what they should attend to and learn, students are led to feel responsible for their own actions. Self-responsibility has implications for children's moral development as well as cognitive development. By taking responsibility for their own participation in Unison Reading groups, children become motivated to be involved, to adhere to the rules of engagement, and to proactively monitor their involvement and progress. In short, because they learn to care more deeply about the things they are responsible for, they make progress in becoming more competent readers.

Rachel Goren, a third-grade teacher, explains how the opportunity to take responsibility for leadership in reading groups has influenced her children's growth as readers. She explains:

I guess also the way the kids really stand up and become leaders is so interesting to me. Even my biggest struggler is so invested in his reading because when he's reading in a Unison group he wants everybody to know he can do it. He gets stuck only when they get stuck. It forces the strugglers to truck ahead and push on. They all want to be the leader and they want their friends to know they can do it.

And the experience of being a leader influences their independent work. For example, at the beginning of the school year when we had just started Unison Reading and I had just introduced the job of the leader, Mia asked if she could be a leader of her own group. I watched her in her group that day and how she took the things she learned in Unison Reading and used them to run her group. As a leader, she led all the breaches. She asked the questions. And the other students were so excited. They wanted to be in her group because she made it positive and happy. From there they all started forming their own groups during independent reading time. They would finish their own books together and do projects together. They were very excited and invested. I feel like Unison Reading gave them the opportunity to learn how to be leaders and the desire to want to use that role independently. And because of that they became independent and more successful. They were more invested and excited about their reading. They were all stepping up to that role. It made them excited, and they wanted to do it.

Adhering to Rules: An Example From a Special Education Class

Unison Reading relies on explicit rules to make sure that everyone has a clear understanding of self-responsibility and so that all group members can hold one another accountable. The rules are firm and nonnegotiable. But they are also simple and unobtrusive.

The rules of Unison Reading create a wide enough space for children to have the freedom to explore their own ideas through dialog. In the following example, Kerry Rutishauser, the principal of the Jacob Riis School, comments on the power of the Unison Reading method to hold the students in a self-contained special education setting accountable for their own learning. Although principal, Kerry regularly teaches a group of eighth-grade boys in a self-contained classroom (meaning the school is mandated to provide a classroom setting in which the student to teacher ratio is no more than 12:1). The self-contained special education program was restructured in order to reintegrate students back into certain general education classes. Rather than spending the full school day in the 12:1 setting, students spend a partial day in the 12:1 class, where they participate in daily Unison Reading sessions and receive academic assistance where necessary. They are able to join the general education classes in most subjects contingent upon their ability to participate consistently in Unison Reading and to keep up with work assigned in the general education classroom. Kerry comments about her involvement with the five boys in the eighth-grade self-contained classroom:

In Unison Reading they have to breach. It's a rule. So when they're not breaching, there are ways you let them know that. When you're taking notes on the Unison Reading Record, you can let the kids see the Record and say, "Look I just want to do a little process check here. I want to show you how things went. Isaac, look, you breached three times. Jaric, look at how your column is empty. You didn't participate. And Devon, you were participating, but you didn't breach the group. So what's going on?" I often do these process checks at the end, because it helps build a student's self-awareness and sense of competency. It's feedback that allows students to set goals for improvement. "Let's look at our records here and see how things went. How much did you breach and participate?"

There was one session where there was a lot of dysfunction. Isaac and Joe were doing all the talking, and Devon and Jaric weren't talking at all. They had all previously agreed to participate, so I gave them consequences for not living up to their commitments. There are rules of Unison Reading we have all agreed to follow. So, for not participating, Devon and Jaric accumulated consequences in our session. They had to serve detention with me, miss electives, and miss [going into the general education] class. Of course, right before I was about to give them the last consequence for not participating, which was a call home, Jaric and Devon decided they were going to participate. Toward the end of Unison Reading they participated. I showed them the record.

Over time, the kids become conscious of their participation in the group and they care about it. For example, Isaac, because I have that Record, wants to make sure when he does something promotive or breaches the group that I write it down—verbatim. So revealing the Record to them is really helpful because they see their competence building over time. That's competence feedback right there. "Let's look at the Unison Reading work and see how you did." Just by doing that some kids will see blanks, and then next time they'll do better because they don't like to see their column blank. But some kids, like Devon and Jaric, I had to give consequences to. "This is the third time you haven't followed the rules of Unison Reading, and there are consequences."

When the kids are learning the protocol, I frequently stop the group and just do a process check to let them know how they are doing. "When you turned around and said, 'what do you think?' to him, that was really promotive." And, "That's really good that you did that." Or, "You stopped the group twice. You noticed somebody wasn't reading." You just have to let them know what they're doing well. I do that a lot at the beginning with all the Unison Reading groups I taught. But you don't have to do that once they start rolling and see the value in participating together and coming to a common understanding of what things mean.

Taking notes is really important for many reasons. One is that it records the teaching, the breaches, the follow in and all the things the kids are saying. You can start to find patterns in what the kids are breaching. But maybe even more importantly, it's a feedback system. The kids really see what they're competent in. They want you to be writing stuff down about them. They like that. I think that's why

(Continued)

(Continued)

Jaric eventually came around—it feels good when you're participating and saying smart things. It's taken him a while to participate. At the beginning of the year he often refused to participate; and he would never volunteer to be group leader. But just like three weeks ago he started to be group leader. He still won't stop when he comes to a word he doesn't know. He still won't breach the group. But he's participating. In a conference I had with him (this is how the conferences support growth), he said, "I still need to work on decoding." I said, "Really? Whenever you come to a word you can't decode in Unison Reading you never stop the group!" He's like, "Yeah, maybe I need to do that." I'm like, "Yeah, so why don't we make that a rule?" I laugh at the irony. He's like, "OK." Then he laughs, realizing the need to follow the rule.

Participating in the Group Process:
An Example From an Inclusive Sixth-Grade Class

In Unison Reading all members of the group experience the same reading process, providing an engaging social situation in which children of varying abilities and experiences join together to read texts and discuss text features and ideas. This protocol creates a context for texts to become the object of joint critical appraisal, supporting the development of comprehension (understanding what is read), metalinguistic awareness (insights about how language works), and metacognition (awareness of how their thinking works). In the following example, Amy Piller explains how participating in Unison Reading leads to learning.

I teach sixth-grade social studies and English in a combined general education/special education classroom. On a nationally standardized reading comprehension assessment, my students score in a range from the 2nd to the 99th percentile. Practicing Unison Reading is what unites these statistically segregated kids, and fundamentally what creates a space for those scoring in the low range to feel like they have a place and a purpose in the classroom. I taught reading for years without Unison Reading, and painfully watched struggling readers give up, tune out, and loose faith in their potential. I am so grateful for having learned this curriculum because I feel like I'm teaching reading for the first time, instead of instituting classroom management to create a silent environment, merely enabling those who were already good readers to get more practice.

One of my earliest memories of Unison Reading has to do with the word *merely*, which I just casually used to conclude my last paragraph. It's words like this that Unison Reading has helped me realize that struggling readers don't know and gloss over, ultimately creating unresolved confusion. For this Unison Reading session, Eddy chose an article about the video game *Batman: Arkham Asylum* from "GamePro," magazine. Although thrilled by the pictures, the written content would have been too complicated for Eddy to read independently, and had he tried, would have resulted in the all-too-familiar image, of the child flipping through the magazine, enjoying himself but not getting the practice teachers crave. Luckily, Eddy chose the article for Unison Reading, and from the first sentence the aforementioned act of true practice came into effect. It read, "While other superheroes merely catch the crooks and then parade around with smug smirks, Batman goes out of his way to get inside the criminal mind and twist it into submission; that alone makes him one of my favorite comic book characters." The group stopped first to figure out *merely*, meaning they had only read the first four words of the sentence. Robby suggested we get rid of the "ly" to see if we knew the beginning of the word, but no one in the group did, so James suggested that we read on. That led to a discussion of the use of the word *parade* and a discussion of some wrestling references to clarify the idea of submission. Jeremy then said he thought we had read enough that we needed to go back and figure out merely. Someone started to search for it in the dictionary when James had a revelation. He said that he thought because the sentence started with the word while, that the second half of the sentence had to be different than the first. When questioned a little by his group mates, he said he meant that the second half would be the opposite of the first and that since Batman does all of this crazy stuff, merely probably meant just doing enough to get by. Everybody reread and agreed that this made sense. The dictionary definition that they found, which previously would have meant little more than a gobbledygook of complicated words, now also was something they could understand. With confidence, they plodded on to the next sentence, and the next.

Over and over again I have watched Unison Reading provide moments like these where light bulbs go off and kids learn from one another. Instead of snapping at kids for feeling frustrated and therefore getting distracted during silent, independent reading, I'm now eliciting their questions and comments in a social reading setting that they want to participate in. I find it to be miraculous!

Unison Reading emphasizes the reader's stance as a member of a group relating to a common text as much as it does a concern for intramental processes of decoding and comprehending. While the latter are factors traditionally associated with reading instruction and development, and have become the taken-for-granted content of all reading curricula, within the context of Unison Reading these competencies are seen merely as ways of thinking and doing things with texts that get passed among group members along relational pathways. Because the success of Unison Reading depends upon the group process, the way that children do and do not uphold their obligations as members of a group so that conversations are worthwhile becomes the pedagogical focus. The emergence of reading competencies, such as decoding and comprehending, for example, depend on social competencies. Intellectual achievements normally associated with literacy are the products of successful interaction in learning groups where reading is practiced.

GETTING STARTED WITH UNISON READING ■

Now that you have an idea of how Unison Reading works, plan a session in your classroom with one group of children. Carefully reread the vignettes featured in this chapter. Take notes on the points you want to be sure to raise in your Unison Reading group.

1. Select children to form a small group of three students who will be at ease with you and each other and willing to read aloud.

2. Plan two 20–30 minute Unison Reading sessions during the first few days of the week.

3. Enlist the help of group members in finding an appealing text no longer than six to eight paragraphs, such as a short feature article written for an audience of children their age. Make sure the text is ENTICING! Finding a text that is highly interesting will make your Unison Reading dreams come true. Help them find a text that will make kids giggle, gasp, or argue. A true test if you've succeeded is when children outside the group ask, "Can I read it next?"

4. Make one copy of the text for each child and one for yourself.

5. Photocopy a Unison Reading Record for your use during the group (one first page and multiple second pages; see Figure 1.4 or go to www.unisonreading.com).

6. Bring something to write on—a white board, notepad, or scrap paper. In response to teaching points that arise, you'll need this material to do word work or diagram ideas.

7. Begin the first session by giving each child in the group a copy of the text.

8. Review Unison Reading ground rules: Read together in sync, read audibly so that your group mates can hear you, and speak up when you are confused or have something to share. And don't be bored!

9. Ask, "Okay, where shall we begin?" If it is a feature article, they will have options—the title, picture captions, bi-lines, section headings. You need to let the children propose to one another how to begin. You can facilitate their decision-making process, but don't make the decisions for them. If they turn to you for the answer, reply, "It's your group, what do you think?"

10. Get them started. You might ask, "How are we going to get ourselves started?" You can ask if anyone wants to be group leader, and ask them to get you started. Group leaders will typically find a way to set the pace. Some children count: one, two, ready, go. . . .

11. In most classrooms, children are trained to raise their hands to be called on by the teacher. It is important from the beginning to instruct children not to raise their hands, but to learn to address one another. You might need to teach into the etiquette of turn taking. If one child dominates, you might need to discuss how to balance conversational turns and mention everyone's responsibility not only to speak up a fair share of the time, but to allow the space for others to speak up. If they continually appeal to you for assistance or approval, look away in order to force them to assume responsibility for sustaining the conversation. Try to focus your attention on note taking without looking up to the group. This will encourage their agency in the conversation.

12. Until children grow comfortable and accustomed to stopping the group, you might need to step in and give a hand. "Ooops, we need to stop because I don't hear everyone reading." Or, "Hold on, one of you said 'completed' and another said 'complicated.' Which word do you like? Why?"

13. During the introductory sessions, you'll find yourself interrupting the group more than the children. You need to bring this to their attention. "Notice how I'm always the one stopping the group? That needs to be your responsibility. Remember, if you have something to say or want to talk about a feature in the text, say, 'hold on!'"

14. Occasionally stop and do some processing. "I want you to notice something. Look at what a great conversation we had about climate change, and all because Devin stopped the group to say he didn't know the word *displacement.* Look how much we can all learn when you have the courage to raise your questions with the group!"

15. Record what each child says as they contribute to the group discussion. Help the children to notice how their contributions support rich conversations. Be careful, though, not to signal that contributing is a competition.

16. Make sure that the children speak to each other, and not to you. If they habitually look at you when they make a comment, you can gesture them to address their peers or nonchalantly cast your gaze toward the table, forcing them to address one another.

17. Remember to take notes. Once a child miscues or stops the group, code the breach/insight by domain. In the column beneath the child's name, record any

details worth noting. In the far right column, record details of the discussion including significant instructional points.

18. When time has run out, stop the group and ask, "How did it go? What did you think?" Children tend to have good insights about the group process. When they do, acknowledge them, and ask how the insights can feed back into the process the next time the group meets. Record their commitments, about which you should remind the students at the beginning of their next meeting.

19. Take a few minutes to reflect on the experience. Look over the Record. What did you learn about your students as readers? What do you think they learned about themselves as readers? What aspects of the experience were easy? Difficult? How will you do things differently next time?

If this is your first experience with Unison Reading, you are bound to have many questions. In the spirit of Unison Reading, I suggest you use your questions to guide your learning. Begin by taking a look at some questions I've collected (see Figure 1.13) that are commonly asked by teachers who are new to Unison Reading. And before reading further, you may want to take stock of your own questions. This book is written to address these questions. More detailed information about implementing Unison Reading throughout your classroom is provided in Chapter 2. Chapter 3 offers an account of the logic behind Unison Reading practices. And Chapter 4 addresses many of these questions through the accounts of teachers who implement Unison Reading in their classrooms.

Figure 1.13 Teachers' Common Questions About Unison Reading

Delayed Readers: Don't delayed readers get frustrated in heterogeneous reading groups? What happens to the "nonreaders" or those children who can't read many words? Does Unison Reading cause delayed readers to be embarrassed?

Advanced Readers: Doesn't the slow pace of reading inhibit the development of advanced readers? Are they bored by the slow pace of Unison Reading? How does Unison Reading benefit advanced readers?

Younger Children: Unison Reading used with emergent readers seems similar to guided reading. In what ways is Unison Reading distinctive?

Older Children: How do you introduce Unison Reading groups to older children who resist reading aloud together with peers? How can Unison Reading be justified at the middle and high school levels when children need practice reading silently?

English Language Learners: How does Unison Reading support English language learners? How can I be sure that English language learners receive the explicit instruction they need to learn English literacy?

Children With Special Needs and Dispositions: How does Unison Reading support children with ADHD? Don't these children distract others in their groups? How realistic is Unison Reading for children with speech problems such as stuttering or language processing delays? How is Unison Reading helpful to children with varying forms of autism? How are they helped to participate in the group process? How do I support the child who is timid or shy? Isn't Unison Reading detrimental to shy children or those who lack confidence and self-esteem?

Student Independence: What happens in groups when the teacher is not present? How realistic is it to expect children to stay "on task" when they facilitate their own groups?

(Continued)

| Figure 1.13 | (Continued) |

Peer Dynamics: What happens when children select groups because of friendships instead of text choices? How do I deal with bullying, teasing, and other aggressive behaviors? How do I prevent children from using Unison Reading groups to reinforce cliques and exclude unpopular children? How do I help children break free of peer pressure in order to express their own ideas? How does the experience of participating in Unison Reading influence the child's sense of identity? What strategies can be used to encourage the formation of groups of children with mixed abilities?

Formal Instruction: Is it appropriate to pre-teach topics such as main idea, vocabulary, or purpose? Does the teacher ever select the reading material? Does Unison Reading "work" in the traditional sense of building the child's decoding and comprehension abilities? How?

Unison Reading Within the Reading Curriculum as a Whole: How is Unison Reading integrated with an existing reading curriculum? How can I accommodate Unison Reading within an already tight reading curriculum?

Parent's Concerns: How can I reassure concerned parents that Unison Reading benefits their children?

Administrator's Concerns: How can I convince my principal to support the Unison Reading program?

Cost Effectiveness: How costly is Unison Reading to implement relative to other instructional programs?

Teacher's Skill: This program seems to require a great deal of skill on the part of the teacher to address nonacademic, socioemotional behaviors and to manage the power dynamics of peer relationships. Are these expectations realistic for teachers who are not trained in counseling?

■ CONCLUSION: "CHEW FOOD TASTE BETTER"

A group of three fifth-grade students had just finished reading a few paragraphs of a feature article on global warming. It was their first encounter with the Unison Reading process, and I asked, as I usually do on such occasions, for the children to reflect on the process—how did reading together and talking about the reading affect the process? The children commented that the process was slower than is usually the case in reading groups, but they understood more. Chen, an English language learner whose native language is Chinese, agreed, "Like eating: Chew food taste better." Chen offers a perfect metaphor for Unison Reading. Like sharing a meal with friends, Unison Reading allows children to savor words as they would delectable morsels. Food, like words, tastes better when you take time to chew.

Unison Reading involves all members of a small group in a joint reading process of the same text, bringing to communal consciousness any aspect of the text that caused confusion for one of its members and allowing for communal critical analysis and understanding. Individual understanding develops through opportunities to think about things like letters, sounds, symbols, ideas, and even personal behaviors in reference to the way that others in their groups think about these things.

Unison Reading is a highly oral process relying on children to read out loud and to be willing to speak up about the things that confuse or intrigue them as processes that scaffold learning. The logic for this highly oral process is that children rely on extensive exposure to oral discourses to make sense of texts independently. The practice of Unison Reading provides a way to bridge the divide between orality and literacy by putting reading into a highly social, oral context with the understanding that children are at a significant advantage when they have opportunities to read socially and learn from others. Unison Reading is a method that attends to both the social and the cognitive processes involved in reading.

The Unison Reading method offers a framework for a simple, functional classroom routine that is inclusive of all children, involving them as participants in textual collectives where literacy competencies are a product of their social involvement. Every Unison Reading episode gives each participant an opportunity to define what literacy means at that particular point in time, addressing the questions "Why are we reading this? How should it best be read? What does it mean?"

What is most significant about Unison Reading is not the particular skills or bits of knowledge that each child takes away, but the experience of having practiced the dispositions and habits of mind required in the role of reader within a community of readers. It is precisely these dispositions and habits of mind—rather than a collection of discrete competencies—that enables literacy to be a generative force in the larger trajectory of the child's development.

2

Unison Reading as a Program of Instruction

Classroom Implementation

Unison Reading as a method for group reading instruction was described in the previous chapter. This chapter explains how Unison Reading can also be used as a comprehensive classroomwide program of reading instruction in K–8 classrooms. I present the underlying principles that inform the Unison Reading method as well as an explanation of the model, including strategies for instructional grouping, identifying group leaders, and selecting reading curriculum materials. The procedures involved in implementation are summarized at the end of the chapter.

■ UNISON READING: PRINCIPLES FOR PRACTICE

Unison Reading adheres to a set of principles that determine its routines and methods in implementation. These principles are the following:

- *Equity.* All children deserve instruction provided by the teacher, but Unison Reading adheres to the *fairness principle* of distributive justice (Rawls, 1999): children in greater need of support should receive greater attention sufficient to enable them to meet grade-level learning standards (Gordon, 1999). The true measure of a pedagogy's worth is how well it meets the needs of the most vulnerable students.

- *Maximal instruction.* Every student should receive frequent and consistent instruction through daily reading lessons. Instruction should target students' individual needs and should balance attention to all reading domains. Since the teacher to student ratio in most classrooms creates a challenge for the average teacher to meet this demand, the instructional approach must be structured in such a way as to enable the teacher to provide sufficient instruction.

• *Quality instruction.* Since Unison Reading employs a social definition of reading, reading skills and strategies are understood to emerge from social situations in which reading is used. As a sociocultural method, Unison Reading expands instructional concerns beyond the traditional focus on vocabulary, phonics, comprehension, and fluency—dimensions that play a critical role in reading development (National Reading Panel, 2000)—to incorporate attention to the affective and relational factors that are now recognized to be as consequential to reading development as cognitive factors. In addition to the traditional cognitive factors commonly associated with reading instruction, Unison Reading instruction emphasizes the social processes that occur within a group and the demands made upon the reader based on text genre. These concerns are neglected by most conventional reading instruction approaches.

• *Student engagement, independence, and responsibility.* Learning is most successful when it is enjoyable and allows some degree of autonomy and opportunity to assume responsibility for learning. The reading curriculum should allow children maximum choice in selecting texts, forming working groups, determining when they are confused, and how to resolve their confusions. The reading curriculum should offer students opportunities to set goals for themselves and follow through on their commitments.

• *Teacher agency, independence and expertise.* The experience of teaching should itself foster the development of teacher agency, independence and expertise; and the reading program should be organized to support these traits. First, the program systems and routines should be streamlined enough to be easily used by any teacher, regardless of level of experience. Second, the activities required should involve the teacher in interactions with children that, over time, contribute to a teacher's insight and expertise about reading development. Instructional programs that are extensively technical, overly cumbersome, or highly prescriptive sabotage the development of expertise and professional autonomy. Scripted programs minimize opportunities for teachers to develop agency, independence, and expertise.

• *Economy.* Staggering sums of public funds are spent each year on expensive shrink-wrapped curriculum packages that prescribe a course of reading instruction. The "business" of reading instruction is a multi-billion-dollar-a-year industry. Unison Reading provides a solution to the cycle of expensive outsourcing school systems have come to depend on. The Unison Reading program is not a commodity, but a protocol based on sound principles. It is inexpensive to implement. The basic routines of Unison Reading instruction are intentionally designed to involve children in utilizing print materials that already exist in most classrooms, school libraries, and at home. The Unison Reading program is essentially cost free, allowing funds normally spent on expensive commercial literacy assessment and instruction programs to be reallocated for purchasing children's trade books, encyclopedias, and subscriptions to magazines (see Appendix B for an annotated list of recommended children's magazines: these choices represent the top picks of the teachers and students at the Jacob Riis School).

• *Democracy.* Education, and reading education specifically, plays a fundamental role in ensuring the viability of a democratic society that depends on its educational system to promote the values and practices of civil discourse and safeguard democratic values. Reading is a medium through which ideas can be freely exchanged, promoting the fluid transfer of new ideas and values that have the power to address social problems as they arise. The challenges of an increasingly complex society warrant the pursuit of democratic schooling practices. Ideally, the reading curriculum should

- o support free interaction and communication of experience within the classroom,
- o provide equable opportunities to receive and to take from others within the context of the reading curriculum, and
- o provide a means by which a large variety of undertakings and experiences can be shared.

Unison Reading honors these commitments by supporting a system of grouping and social interaction that is fully integrated and in which children exercise freedom to interact and communicate with the broadest possible range of other individuals. The method abolishes ability and leveled grouping practices on the grounds that learning groups stratified by ability segregate classrooms and defy democratic educational principles.

■ CLASSROOM IMPLEMENTATION

Based on the above principles, I developed the following set of guidelines for implementing Unison Reading as a classroomwide program of instruction:

1. Every child should receive two sessions per week of Unison Reading with a teacher and two sessions that meet independently from the teacher.

2. Children should have the opportunity to choose instructional texts that they wish to read.

3. Effort should be made to encourage diversity of experiences and abilities within the context of instructional groups. Children should not be grouped by ability, as this practice has proven detrimental to minority students (Lleras & Rangel, 2009).

These four guidelines form the basis for implementing the Unison Reading approach. The system of routines and practices outlined in the remainder of this chapter will enable you to begin using Unison Reading in your classroom.

Assessing Reading Level

Though reading levels are not relevant for instructional purposes within the Unison Reading approach, it is nonetheless important to obtain baseline assessment data and to monitor children's progress. Begin by assessing children for their reading level. I recommend a *Blitzkrieg* approach that can be completed on all children in a classroom over the course of a single reading period or two. The goal is to gather data on every student as quickly as possible without using valuable instructional time. At the Jacob Riis School, where Unison Reading was piloted, the Dynamic Indicators of Basic Emergent Literacy Skills (DIBELS; University of Oregon, n.d.) is used in Grades K–1, and the Degrees of Reading Power (Questar Assessment, 2000) is used in Grades 2–8. DIBELS has shortcomings as an early literacy assessment, primarily due to an overbearing emphasis on oral reading speed and accuracy in first grade, which the Unison Reading program does not emphasize. In spite of its shortcomings, the data generated from the DIBELS provide a snapshot of the general progress our primary students make in mastering fundamental reading skills. And since the assessment is quick to administer, we are able to preserve instructional time. But alternative assessments can be used for *Blitzkrieg* assessment, including Measures of Academic Progress (MAP; Northwest Evaluation Association, 2003) and Scholastic Reading Inventory (SRI; Scholastic, 2006). I specifically discourage the use of informal reading inventories as benchmarking systems, as they are cumbersome to administer and drain substantial amounts of instruction from the curriculum. These assessments require one-on-one administration at a rate of 15–20 minutes per child, consuming weeks of valuable instructional time for the purposes of assessment. A quick benchmarking assessment will help you identify children according to need. The data typically provided by the informal reading inventory, such as running records of oral reading and prompts to probe comprehension, are collected in the context of one-on-one conferences, a routine format within the Genre Practice model.

Ranking Children by Need

In order to be accountable to those in greatest need, you must know who they are. Use the Instructional Priority List in Appendix A to rank order children for instructional

| Figure 2.1 | Sample Instructional Priority List, Second Grade (Children Ranked by National Percentile Score on the Degrees of Reading Power Assessment in Order of Lowest to Highest) |

Instructional Priority List

List children's names in order of priority as determined by diagnostic assessment score.

First-Level Students	SCORE	Second-Level Students	SCORE
1 Wu, H.	22	6 Lopez, J.	25
2 Arnez, A.	25	7 Martinez, L.	25
3 Flores, E.	25	8 Chia, A.	25
4 Huang, L.	25	9 Williams, L.	25
5 Johnson, D.	25	10 Wang, G.	25

Third-Level Students	SCORE	Fourth-Level Students	SCORE
11 Davis, M.	30	16 Lan, K.	69
12 Liu, M.	48	17 Encarnacion, A.	71
13 Shi, C.	57	18 Baragon, O.	72
14 Wu, L.	62	19 Anthony, M.	75
15 Yang, J.	64	20 Li, H.	79

(Continued)

Figure 2.1 (Continued)

Third-Level Students	SCORE	Fourth-Level Students	SCORE
21 Wang, Y.	79	26	
22 Martinez, J.	84	27	
23		28	
24		29	
25		30	

priority based on results from progress monitoring assessments. Children with the greatest need for instruction are ranked in the first level, and those with the least need are ranked in the lowest level. (See Figure 2.1 for an example of how the Instructional Priority List was used in a second-grade classroom.) Identify the child who received the lowest score on Line #1 (your first priority), and rank order children in order of lowest to highest scores. Students should not have access to this form. This is for your reference only.

Scheduling Groups

Unison Reading groups meet four times per week, for 15–20-minute sessions. (Some middle school teachers hold Unison Reading groups for 30-minute slots.) Two sessions are held with a teacher, and two are held independently.

The number of Unison Reading slots depends on the number of children in the classroom. In a hypothetical classroom of 25 students, five slots are created and labeled A–E (see Figure 2.2 for example). These slots will remain stable from week to week. You will teach two Unison Reading groups per day. Every child will participate in one Unison Reading group, four days a week.

Within the Genre Practice model, Unison Reading groups take place within the Reading Block which lasts anywhere from 60–80 minutes. Typically, groups begin after a brief lesson that initiates the Block. Unison Reading groups meet for the first 30–40 minutes of a 60–80 minute reading block (one group every 15–20 minutes). Keep a timer to remind you when to end one group and begin the next (you can give yourself more than 15–20 minutes when you are learning the method). Though it's tempting to let groups run overtime, is critical to stay on schedule so as to ensure that all groups receive equal instructional opportunity.

When you first start using this approach, you will need to plan to teach procedures and expectations for Unison Reading during the lesson time of the reading block. Children need to understand that they must work quietly, move about the room without distracting others, and keep their materials organized so as not to delay the already-tight meeting schedule.

Identifying Group Leaders

Select children from the third or fourth level on the Instructional Priority List to be the first set of group leaders (I recommend this method of assigning group leaders to insure

Figure 2.2	Weekly Unison Reading Schedule for Groups With and Without Teacher, Ariel Ricciardi's Fourth-Grade Classroom

Unison Reading Schedule

	Monday	Tuesday	Wednesday	Thursday	Friday
Teacher	Group C (D) Group D (R) Group E (R/D)	Group A (D) Group B (R)	Group A (D) Group B (R)	Group C (D) Group D (R) Group E (R/D)	
Independent		Group C Group D Group E	Group C Group D Group E	Group A Group B	Group A Group B

that the lowest- and highest-functioning readers are dispersed across groups). Alternatively, you can use a class list or some other system of assigning leadership roles. Group leaders will help initiate the Unison Reading program by being the first to select texts for groups to read.

Group leadership rotates so that every child has an equal opportunity to be a leader. Do not use leadership opportunities as a reward, a practice that will sabotage motivation in children who never receive rewards and instill the desire to lead for all the wrong reasons in children who readily receive them. Group leader roles are equally distributed because all children benefit by having the opportunity to hone their leadership talents. Each week a new set of leaders is identified from a different level of the Instructional Priority List. In a class of 25 students where it has been determined that five groups meet each week, five students are assigned the role of group leader each week, and every child assumes the role of group leader once during the course of each five-week cycle.

In addition to selecting the group's text, a group leader is responsible for bringing materials to the group (folders with copies of the selected text, dictionary) and calling group members together for meetings. Group leaders are taught to be attentive to the group process and help facilitate the discussion to make sure that all children participate. On days the group meets independent of the teacher, leaders are responsible for keeping the schedule. Because the Unison Reading protocol is simple, once it is learned, most children are able to facilitate the reading with only limited adult support. Don't let children skip their leadership responsibilities. Important lessons are learned when the child has responsibility for the group, not only about reading but also about life in general.

"I find Unison reading to be extremely helpful with my ELLs. I have a little girl in my class who is learning English and is very shy. In the beginning of the year she was able to decode the words but I wasn't sure if she was able to comprehend what she was reading. She was hesitant to answer my questions. However, once she had the opportunity to be the group leader and hold the other students in the group accountable, she began to relish her leadership role and began to feel more comfortable in speaking out in the group. She loves to lead, help her friends, and answer questions in the comfort of the small group. She has recently begun to ask questions of her classmates when something doesn't make sense to her or when she doesn't know the word in English in order to explain what she wants to say." Barry Greenberg, first-grade teacher.

Selecting Texts

A distinctive feature of the Unison Reading program is that children themselves are responsible for selecting texts for groups to read.

The system of text selection begins with the assignment of weekly group leaders, as described above. Group leaders are responsible for selecting a text that would be appealing for others. This process usually requires the involvement of the teacher, depending on the age of the children and how familiar children are with the process of selecting texts with other readers in mind (something children are not usually accustomed to thinking about). Younger children require greater teacher assistance in selecting texts. Second graders, for example, rely on the teacher to suggest suitable texts. Children in upper elementary and middle school are more able to choose suitable texts independently, but still need to consult with the teacher in order to take into account whether the text is accessible and can practically be read in a week. Some children invariably choose texts that are too difficult to be enjoyable. If a text seems too challenging, I usually try to engage the child in a discussion about the appropriateness of the text. If they insist on moving forward with a text I believe is inappropriate, I suggest a back-up text in case their group later decides to abandon the first text.

During the Unison Reading meeting, when symptoms of misguided text choices present themselves as breaches (such as too many stops that kill the momentum), I engage the children in a conversation to help them identify the elements of the text that are causing difficulty and to think about strategies for text selection to support better choices in the future. In such cases, feel free to breach the group: "You seem bored and frustrated. Is this text too hard to be any fun? Then what do you want to do about it?" It's ok to let children know that they can abandon the text for a more appropriate one, if they agree as a group. Then help them think about what to read for their remaining sessions of the week.

In Pre-K, kindergarten, and during the first half of first grade, group leaders select two little books for their group to read during the week, and both titles are listed on the sign up sheet. By the middle of first grade, especially in classrooms where teachers have exposed children to a range of generic forms of texts, children begin to select different genres, and a text can easily extend over the period of a week (for example, the first-grade advice column from *Highlights Magazine*).

Student choice in text selection is a fundamental tenet of the Unison Reading approach, accomplishing these important objectives:

- Giving children agency and responsibility to select texts that will be appealing and interesting to peers
- Insuring that the content of the reading curriculum is engaging to children
- Unburdening teachers from having to manage a process of materials selection for a student-centered curriculum
- Involving children in a powerful form of critical thinking because the process affords them the opportunity to think about texts in relation to the way they anticipate others will engage with texts

Teacher guidance and support

Selecting a text for a group to read, especially when you don't know who, exactly, will be in the group, is itself an exercise in comprehension. This responsibility asks the child to invoke theory of mind capacities: that unique human ability to think about something in a way that anticipates how another person will think about that thing (Astington, Harris, & Olson, 1988; Olson, 2007). Every time it is their turn to select a text as group leader children have opportunities to pose questions to themselves such as, what does this text accomplish? How well does it work? How will my group respond? Because selecting the text for a group forces a heightened level of critical reading, being group leader is a powerful reading exercise. The text selection procedure provides a context for teachers to foster children's critical reading stance. For example, teachers in upper elementary and middle school create opportunities for children to get feedback from classmates on the quality of texts selected. This practice helps build the capacity to consider how their selections might resonate with others, a practice that requires students to engage the higher-order cognitive capacities known as executive functioning.

Children new to Unison Reading who have had texts chosen for them and who have not been allowed to exercise autonomy and responsibility in making informed reading choices will tend to select texts impulsively: a topic of high personal interest, but with overly challenging syntax or vocabulary or insipid content; too short to hold interest over time; or too long to complete. Children who have previously been exposed to a teacher-directed curriculum and who are not highly motivated or self-aware readers will initially lack a sense of agency. They may lack awareness or have little to no regard for their peers' reading interests and preferences. Initially, it is difficult to consider the potential of a text to satisfy the interests of others.

The process of text selection may require a little coaching. During independent work time, plan to meet with next week's group leaders, either individually or together. Guide them to consider the features and potential of the text in relation to anticipated response.

Texts are chosen based on general appeal and the understanding that they can be read over the course of four meetings in a week. The content that lends itself well to Unison Reading sessions includes short feature articles (politics, entertainment, sports), short stories, comics, and reviews. So children (with guidance from teachers) select short, whole texts from a broad variety of sources (short news features, sports stories, gossip columns, game reviews, obituaries, sections from content textbook chapters) or shorter segments of texts that make unusual demands on readers such as technical, scientific expository texts or narratives with complex grammar and arcane vocabulary. (See Figure 2.3 for a sample of texts chosen by first through eighth graders.)

The mindset for text selection fosters critical reading skills that should, over time, become detachable so that students are able to approach any text encountered with other perspectives in mind. Children should show signs that they are taking their responsibilities seriously by bringing things to read that they might find outside of school or, by middle school, selecting texts that will allow them to benefit from others' perspectives (for instance, an exemplar text of a genre they are writing or an excerpt of an assigned text for another class). Where previously the school reading curriculum concerned itself with the need to help children gain familiarity of a narrow range of texts that exhibited a fixed set of conventions, today children need to learn how to critically read a broad range of text forms and other symbolic modalities with flexibility, creativity, competence, and purpose in order meet twenty-first-century literacy demands. The Unison Reading text selection protocol provides autonomy for students to sample a broad range of texts.

You are probably already getting a sense of how the very process of text collecting requires children to simultaneously think about their relationship to texts while speculating about the responses of others. In addition to serving as a very practical means of generating curriculum materials, the practice of text collecting has its own inherent pedagogical potential. The active process of searching and sampling texts gives children the opportunity to deliberate about the meanings, merits, and features of texts and to

Figure 2.3   List of Sample Texts Collected, by Grade

Grade 1: Recipe
       Flier for school talent show
       Highlights advice column
       Little books

Grade 2: Science feature on King Tut
       Directions for a science experiment from a children's magazine
       Encyclopedia entry: President Lincoln

Grade 3: State ELA exam excerpt
       Science feature on bird migration
       Dinosaur encyclopedia entry

Grade 4: Sports statistics feature
       Time for Kids news feature on President Obama
       SpongeBob comic
       Pet care feature

Grade 5: Calvin and Hobbs comic
       Magazine feature on global warming
       Science experiment
       Recipe: How to make blood (Halloween)

Grade 6: Sports feature on baseball star Rodriguez
       Short story (ghost story)
       Game review

Grade 7: News feature on recycling
       Gossip article on pop star Taylor Swift
       Sports feature

Grade 8: Tupac Shakur rap lyrics
       Social studies text excerpt on the Cold War
       News feature: Small town bans baggy jeans
       Feature article on dyslexia and ADHD

anticipate how other readers might respond. This seemingly simple cognitive combination is the fundamental essence of comprehension—engaging with the intentions of the writer and speculating about their power to engage with the intentions of the reader. Thinking about how others think about texts is essentially the heart of critical literacy. Text selection is not merely a housekeeping concern, but a process that is full of rich learning potential.

The rule of whole texts

The weekly Unison Reading cycle observes the rule of "whole texts." The texts children select should be short enough to be able to be read, from start to finish, within the four, 15-minute sessions. The rule of whole texts is a solution to a logistical challenge. Unison Reading operates on a tight weekly schedule, and texts must be short in order for the system to function to allow a Unison Reading group to complete the process by the end of the week.

But the rule of whole texts also stems from some basic principle having to do with the way that language works. A text, like any other language "utterance," is an expression of the writer's intentions and serves a specific social purpose (see Bakhtin, Holquist, & Emerson, 1986; Grice, 1989). Writers compose texts with readers in mind, and when doing so, employ specific writing conventions to facilitate communication—conventions that are used in the cultural spheres in which texts are read. This is why, for example, sports writers use language differently than gossip columnists. When reading, there's more to a text than that which meets the eye. Marks on the page can't be interpreted in isolation from the social rules and conventions that govern how the marks should be interpreted. The deeper, implied meanings of texts require the reader to take into consideration the larger situational context of a text in order to comprehend it (Grice, 1989). A reader's familiarity with the cultural sphere aids interpretation of the text. Unison Reading groups provide an interpretive cultural medium in which whole texts are read on a weekly basis. Written genres, such as advice columns, recipes, political ads, or game reviews, possess a sense of wholeness characterized by the ways in which all elements function to accomplish the writer's overall purpose. Word choice, grammar, text organization, structure, and punctuation all work in synchrony to elicit an intended response (in reader or listener).

The Unison Reading cycle allows the group to read the whole text from start to finish, providing the opportunity to consciously consider the way in which all of its parts contribute to the whole meaning. Proficient readers make judgments about an author's overall intent by analyzing the connections between all of the features of a text. Through Unison Reading, readers at all levels of development have important opportunities to learn how to be critical readers through participation with others. By the end of the school year, each child will have had the opportunity in Unison Reading groups to read from 30–40 complete texts across a wide range of genres, providing ample genre practice. The sheer quantity of texts encountered in groups is a distinctive feature of Unison Reading, compared to conventional reading programs that cover sometimes as few as a half dozen genres per year.

The texts children read in their Unison Reading groups should be collected in a binder. Over time, a portfolio of text experiences serves as material evidence of reading identity. At the conclusion of a Unison Reading session in late May, Ella, a first grader, proudly announced to me, "Now I have 18 texts in my binder!" Children often reread texts from their collections during independent reading time. As children reread their text collections, they have an opportunity to reconsider their relationship to the texts and the experiences they represent.

Joining Groups

The weekly routine of signing up for Unison Reading groups by interest represents more than mere logistics. The process involves each child acting as an agent in developing their own reading identity.

As the previous section illustrated, the system of student-initiated text selection is a built-in procedure for grouping students, and there is no need for the teacher to further organize grouping procedures. The process of signing up for a group begins the week prior to the designated Unison Reading cycle. Once group leaders have identified their text, they are presented for consideration to the class as a whole in one of the two following ways:

- Texts are sometimes presented during a reading lesson by the teacher or children themselves. This method allows teachers into engage the whole class in productive conversations about the features of particular texts.
- Texts are posted on a bulletin board. Children can browse the options and sign up during assigned periods. This method is time efficient and does not require whole-class time.

Most children need time to browse and consider which text they want to read, and the independent work time segment of the reading block provides children with ample time to make decisions. Groups are formed for a variety of reasons, having little to do with the child's ability level or gradient of text "difficulty." Children are encouraged to form groups of their own based on mutual interest. Children in Lauren Casion's fifth-grade classroom are called by table to the front of the room to peruse text selections. Once they make their choices they deposit Popsicle sticks labeled with their names into envelopes adjacent to their text choice (see Figure 2.4). Students in Tara Clark's first-grade classrooms record their names on sign-up sheets on clipboards posted in the classroom (see Figure 2.5).

Occasionally you'll find that children might gravitate to groups out of a motivation to be with friends, especially when first learning the Unison Reading approach. But the large majority of children seek out groups for the primary reason that they want to read the featured text. Also, systematic sign-up procedures limit the possibility that cliques can use groups as shelter as there are only five slots per group and children are called according to some established order. Once the class becomes accustomed to the Unison Reading experience and is comfortable participating, children become more at ease participating with all of their peers and the influence of cliques in the classroom diminishes. Essentially,

Figure 2.4   Fifth-Grade Students Browse Text Selections Before Signing Up for Unison Reading Groups

Figure 2.5	First-Grade Sign-Up Sheet

Group
Unison Reading Sign-Up

Group Leader: _Eddie_

Title: _Highlights Advice Column "Secrets"_

Sign-up:

1. _Maria_

2. _Michael_

3. _____

4. _____

children gain the strength and confidence to join groups independently without feeling the need to sign up with friends.

You are what you read: Development of reading identity

Assuming the role of group leader allows every child to have opportunities to select texts they themselves are interested in and relate to. Opportunities to sign up for texts of choice each week give children opportunities to be agents in the development of their own reading identity. Text selecting is very consequential to children, particularly in upper elementary and beyond when children become increasingly sensitive to the ways in which they are viewed and evaluated by others, and they feel the heat of peer appraisals when they are uncomfortable in their relationship to the text being read. Feeling comfortable with the content of a text is an important factor in the process of a successful learning group where children are expected to expose their questions and confusions. Selecting a text is the first step in the process of forming a relationship to material that contributes to the overall identity the child is developing as a reader.

But the Unison Reading protocol also occasionally provides children the opportunity to move outside their comfort zone when they find themselves in groups reading texts that they would not necessarily choose independently. Children in groups that are the last called to sign up must take one of a few remaining slots. For example, Ralique, a "cool" fourth grader who sports a diamond stud in one ear, was among the last to be called to sign up, and the only slot remaining for him to choose was with a group of girls reading a text on how to make crafts. At the time he was upset, breaking down in tears at his predicament. But his teacher was firm. She told him: rules are rules and you can only join groups where space is available. She reminded him that his group would be the first to sign up the following week. The next day I happened to join Ralique at the table where he sat with his female group mates and participated sociably. On another occasion in the same classroom, Billy was the last to sign up for a text and found himself reading an advice column in which one of the entries dealt with the nuisance of wearing a bra. Situations like these occasionally occur and give children opportunities to cross social boundaries and bend their identities in ways they wouldn't do independently. These opportunities stretch sociocognitive and socioperceptual skills that contribute to the ability to be socially competent and comfortable in a range of contexts (such as multicontextual competency).

We learn important things about ourselves when we are pressed to undertake experiences beyond the boundaries our personal identity imposes. Learning to be comfortable affiliating with a wide range of social groups opens new possibilities for development

Getting Ready

Materials

Help the group leader organize materials for their groups—multiple copies of the text and Unison Reading logs (described below). Come to the Unison Reading group that you are joining prepared with your blank Unison Reading Record. Make sure you bring a white board and marker, a notebook, index cards, or sheets of paper. You will need these as you follow into confusions brought about by words or ideas (e.g., breaking words into phonetic chunks, drawing pictures or diagrams to illustrate ideas).

The physical setting: The table as a teaching tool

One of the ground rules of Unison Reading is that participants can hear one another read aloud audibly without disturbing the rest of the class. It is important for participants to be able to see one another's text in order to follow into text features that become the topic of discussion. Therefore, it is important for groups to work at a table small enough in size for each person to hear the others but large enough so that each participant can rest his or her copy of the text on the table surface to be referenced by others. Large tables make it difficult for children to see one another's texts, and children must speak loudly to be heard. Also, at large tables, the more reluctant children have the space to gravitate away from the group.

Avoid working with children on the carpet, a commonplace custom in many child-centered classrooms. Children are inclined to wiggle around, and it's critical that the text be securely placed in front of each child, in a position that can facilitate joint attention on text features. Fan-like table configurations, which are designed to support teacher-led, small-group meetings, are also not suitable for Unison Reading, as they are designed to facilitate teacher-directed language interactions. With Unison Reading, there is no group hierarchy and every person, including the teacher, assumes a place in the circle.

At the Jacob Riis School, we have tried to make sure that all classrooms are equipped with at least two round tables to accommodate both Unison Reading groups simultaneously. If you don't have access to a round table, a rectangular table will suffice. But make sure you seat yourself at either end of the table so that the children are clustered together and don't need to navigate around you to hear one another read or see one another's text.

Establish a permanent place for Unison Reading groups to run on a regular basis. This helps make transitions less distracting and more efficient. Because Unison Reading groups create a hum of noise, it is important to locate reading tables in corners of the room, if possible, and as far from one another as possible, so as to minimize noise interference.

Facilitating Diverse Learning Groups

Unison Reading prohibits the practice of grouping children by level or ability for instruction. Because children group themselves according to the reading choices they make, any given group can potentially include children from a range of different reading levels. The principles that justify this practice are explained in the next chapter. In this section, I'll give suggestions about how to facilitate groups of children with wide-ranging skill levels in a few common situations.

Young children

In primary classrooms it is common to encounter groups comprised of emergent, beginning, and transitional readers. Usually children at this age spend a large portion of their time in groups just trying to coordinate their behaviors, and a substantial proportion of breaches fall under the Social Processes category. With such diversity in skill level, a large proportion of Decoding breaches will also arise. In most cases, conversation is engaging enough to hold everyone's interest. But on occasion children become impatient with one another. For example, there are, of course, times when a child who reads at a higher level becomes frustrated by the process of having to slow down for a child who is struggling with sight words. Other times children in the group might become impatient with the child who isn't able to maintain focus or follow the rules. Both situations present useful opportunities to teach the importance of patience and support for peers. In some cases, the child who is impatient can benefit from a lesson in patience and tolerance. "You chose to be in the group, and you need to follow the rule: read together and be supportive." This is an important lesson especially for advanced readers whose decoding proficiency outpaces social maturity or their capacity for empathy. When children sign up for groups and you notice a low-functioning reader heading toward a text that is too challenging, it is fine to intervene: "Remember how we talked about the need to pick texts that are fun to read, and that it's more fun when you can read most of the words. Let's give this text a try to see if it's a good pick." (This strategy is discussed more fully in the next section.)

In spite of your best efforts to help children find texts of a suitable challenge, there will be times when a less-proficient reader is in a group reading a text that is too challenging and they tire of breaching the group at every confusion. On these occasions I sometimes let the child whisper read in the wake of the group's oral reading, more or less going along for the ride and completing the text as a shared reading experience. Then I try to find time to discuss with the child the need to select texts that are not too challenging.

The non-English speaker

Another situation where vastly diverse abilities exist in groups is when non-English speakers join the community. Since it is antithetical to the inclusivity principle of Unison Reading to segregate these children from the program, they need special accommodations in Unison Reading groups. Participation levels of non-English speakers can be represented as points on a continuum. *Come along for the ride* means that the ELL is physically part of the group, but not expected to be accountable to the rules of reading aloud and breaching the group. Just being a part of the social experience provides rich enough learning until the child has acquired enough English to participate more fully in oral reading.

The next point on the continuum is *participation with accommodations.* English language learners able to read some words can be supported by the other children in the group who are able to slow down the pace of reading sufficiently enough that the ELL can participate. The group can stop at words they think the ELLs might want or learn or need to know and spend time making sure the words and concepts are understood. For example, I was recently in Ian Lambert's fourth-grade classroom and observed a group with two newcomers who both spoke Chinese. The other children in the group read at a pace that was slower than usual, and stopped at words they thought their non-English speaking group mates might want or need to know. At those points, one child, bilingual in English and Chinese, translated the English word into Chinese, and the ELLs wrote the definitions in the margins of their text. The other children in the group contributed by teaching word meanings by drawing pictures, acting out situations, and exhibiting objects in the room. A primary focus of the group experience was to accommodate the needs of the ELLs. The next day Ian told me the group switched back to the *come along for the ride* point on the continuum so as to allow the group to regain momentum in completing the text. The English language learners in Ian's classroom gained an average of 9 units on the Degrees of Reading Power assessment compared to the national average gain of 4 units.

The stoppers

Then there are children who are "stoppers," who intentionally trip up the group process through negative or passive aggressive behaviors. These students might have high opinions of themselves as readers and low regard for oral reading, which they might view as "babyish." They have been socialized by ability grouping practices and have come to view themselves as "high" readers whose status may be threatened by working with those of lower ability. These children need as much attention and intervention to overcome their negative attitudes as low-functioning readers need attention to the technical challenges of texts and strategies to develop self-confidence and a sense of competence. The inclusion principle of Unison Reading requires that all group members follow the rules. Stoppers are no exception.

Kevin comes to mind. He is an eighth grader who has always been considered a "high reader." When I met with his group, he was in a mischievous mood, posing inane questions and intentionally reading too fast, causing the group to have to stop and recalibrate their pace. I called him out, repeated the rules of Unison Reading and explained their importance. "But it's boring!" he pleaded. I looked him squarely in the eye and responded: "I get that you don't like Unison Reading. But most kids get a lot from it. And when you act this way, the Unison Reading session revolves around what you don't like, and then *that's* what the group has to talk about rather than things that are relevant to others. When you do that, you prevent the group from focusing on things they want or need to talk about. It's not fair to the group that you are taking their attention away from what it is that they chose to read for today."

Negative behaviors should not be tolerated in children because they are destructive to the group. And as much as tradition has forced a concern for the cognitive competencies of reading, social competencies are just as consequential. Negative behaviors and attitudes should be treated as seriously as delayed skills. When you notice them, breach the group and follow in. Subsequent to my meeting with Kevin, I recommended to his teacher and the principal that an intervention be arranged. The format of an intervention will be explained in Chapter 4, but, briefly, it is a meeting involving the child's teachers, guidance counselors, the principal, and the assistant principal, at which the child participates in a conversation to clarify expectations, identify behaviors that defy expectations, and make commitments to change behaviors in ways that will meet expectations. Because the definition of reading competence, according to the Unison Reading model, depends as much on social competence as it does on cognitive competence, maladaptive social behaviors receive corrective attention.

A Unison Reading group offers something for everyone

An overarching lesson all children learn as they participate in diverse learning groups is this: There isn't a person anywhere you can't learn something from. Today someone in your group might be tripping up on a word you know, but tomorrow they will teach you something that you didn't know.

Running Groups and Wrapping Up a Session

The previous chapter explained the protocol to be used during Unison Reading sessions. Throughout the session, try your best to hold children accountable to the rules. Desired behaviors need to be established and secured through consistent practice. If you let the rules slip, it will be challenging to re-establish them later.

Children should be instructed to clear the table except for the text they are reading and something to write with. During reading, once children have figured out tricky words, I instruct them to circle the word for later reference when filling out their Student Logs (explained below). They should not use time in the group writing definitions in the margins of the text. During the last few minutes of the session, plan to engage children in a discussion of their strengths, needs, big ideas, and questions they encountered while reading. This is critical in helping them think about behaviors and actions that have the potential to help them improve as readers and learners.

After they have finished their Unison Reading session, each student fills out a Student Unison Reading Log, an activity that prompts reflection over group accomplishments and goals (see Figure 2.6 for a completed example and blank Student Unison Reading Log in Appendix A for a blank Log). Logs are filled out *after* the Unison Reading session so as to preserve time for the group reading process. On this form, children fill out the title and genre of the text they have read, names of group members, their proudest achievement, their goal for the next meeting, and words that were learned during the session. Using the language of learning to describe their behaviors in the group helps to develop critical insights about their own learning. In that way, not only are children taking responsibility for holding themselves accountable for doing the things that are expected, they are using language to describe their behaviors that help build an awareness of their competencies.

After completing a Unison Reading Log, students file it in their personal Unison Reading Folder. The group leader collects texts from the group members for their next meeting, which is filed in a group folder. After the final meeting of the week, children file their text with the others they have collected throughout the year in their personal Unison Reading text binder. Children are encouraged to reread their Unison Reading text collections during independent reading. This gives them the opportunity to revisit concepts and ideas for a second time and to practice reading fluency.

Unison Reading Through Stages of Development

The view of reading development articulated by Fountas and Pinnell (1996) and founded on developmental theory established by Marie Clay (1991), suggests children begin to emerge as readers at a very young age, progress through the early stages of reading development, and transition into a process of reading characterized by personal purpose and independence (see Figure 2.7). Every classroom contains children at varying points on the developmental continuum, and the inclusion principle of Unison Reading

| **Figure 2.6** | Student Unison Reading Log |

Figure 2.7	Fountas and Pinnell's Reading Development Over Time

Emergent: Uses mostly information from pictures and only some features of print; knows some words.

Early: Increasingly relies on print rather than pictures; increasing control of early reading strategies; demonstrates knowledge of a small number of high frequency words; reads familiar texts with fluency; exhibits self-monitoring behaviors.

Transitional: full control of early strategies; integrates use of reading cues (meaning, structure, visual); knows a large number of high-frequency words; reads fluently with expression and phasing; reads longer and more complex texts.

Self-extending: Uses all information flexibly; solves problems independently; reads for meaning, solves problems independently; reads for different purposes; learns from reading; reads across a variety of written genres.

Source: Adapted from Fountas & Pinnell (1996).

guarantees a diversity of reading levels within each group. With this development continuum in mind, this section provides suggestions for using Unison Reading across developmental levels.

Emergent readers

Children come to school already emergent readers. They are practiced in reading symbols in their environment, though they may have only limited experience with formal writing systems. Some young children are less practiced in functioning in large social groups in which formal rules are observed. Unison Reading in Pre-Kindergarten classrooms emphasizes relational behaviors and helps orient children to the routines of collective, coordinated participation, helping children to synchronize their worlds with others. As children learn the rules of Unison Reading and begin to function in learning groups, they learn to talk together about pictures, words, and letters. They also learn how to learn from one another. While decoding is not emphasized by the teacher, children's attention invariably turns to letter-sound relationships, thus helping to lay a foundation of alphabet and phonics knowledge that is the basis of early reading.

Early readers

It's impossible to follow Unison Reading's number one rule, read aloud in sync, when one can't decipher the text. So emergent and early readers benefit from supportive groups in which they can practice matching spoken words with written words.

Primary school teachers will organize text selection procedures so that they can intervene to guide children to select books at a manageable level of challenge. Working one on one or in small groups to peruse text choices, sampling a page or two, and helping children anticipate the demands of the text will help ensure that lower-functioning readers find their way to satisfying groups.

Until about the middle of first grade, "little books"—short, simple stories or expository texts of 80–100 words—are the primary source of Unison Reading material. Libraries of leveled trade books or homemade language experience books are appropriate material. Midway through first grade, as teachers begin to expose children to other genres, group leaders begin to select other genres for Unison Reading (short feature articles from children's magazines, for example).

Groups can typically read two little books a week in Unison Reading groups. Once beginning readers finish a book in Unison Reading, they put it in their book bag (a gallon size bag with their name on it). Each time they meet in a Unison Reading session, a new book goes into the bag and the oldest one is removed. Each day during the reading block, when they are not in Unison Reading groups, children are expected to read each of the books in their book bag, either independently or to a partner before they go into literacy centers. These opportunities to reread books they have encountered in Unison Reading help secure reading strategies, develop fluency, and secure word recognition abilities.

Transitional readers

Reading in sync is manageable once children reach the beginning to intermediate level. The collective knowledge and social competencies of children at this level enable most groups to function relatively independently, even when there is a large disparity in skill level amongst group members. Unison Reading emphasizes interdependence as opposed to individual performance, and the Unison Reading group situation is forgiving of children who read at a lower level than their peers because rules assure promotive behaviors, insuring the group essentially serves as a scaffold of support to work through points of confusion.

Early readers who are a minority in classrooms of mostly transitional readers might need attention during the text selection process to ensure an appropriate level of challenge.

Self-extending and advanced readers

Students at this stage should begin to use the Unison Reading session to share texts they want to gain perspective about. Unison Reading, with ample space for conflict and dialog, is well suited to the adolescent child's inclination to wrestle with conflicting ideas. Unison Reading groups are especially appropriate for the specialized genres of history, science, and mathematics because the medium of dialog supports deliberation of ideas. In addition to the reading block, the Unison Reading approach can be implemented in content classrooms where teachers can compile binders of unit-related texts. Students can make text choices from these binders, encyclopedias, or textbooks.

Challenges along the developmental continuum

Since Unison Reading depends on children's ability to synchronize their reading process so that they can resolve problems together, learning depends upon successful group interaction. Reading aloud in sync is a rule that forces attention to social competencies. This can be a challenge for children of all ages.

The level of teacher involvement required to help the group function will be relative to the children's developmental level and their previous experience in taking responsibility for the group reading process. Most children of all ages have been taught to raise hands to be acknowledged by teachers for permission to speak. This age-old custom is counterproductive in the context of Unison Reading because it diminishes student autonomy. Hand raising needs to be eliminated immediately if Unison Reading is to function successfully. "You can put your hand down. Go ahead, speak up. Just take turns the way you would when you're talking to your friends." It doesn't take long until children can conduct their own conversations with ease. Kindergarten children are only beginning to solidify their innate capacity to think about things in reference to how they think others think about them. They are also only beginning to learn the **relational** behaviors that enable them to participate in formal conversations. They require support in learning conversational etiquette and socially appropriate practices that enable the exchange of ideas, as shown in the following vignette:

**GLOSSARY BOX:
RELATIONAL**

of or relating to aspects of interpersonal relationships

Three kindergarten boys, all of whom speak English as a second language, are the lowest functioning readers in the classroom. They are Unison Reading a pre-primer book of a few pages. Having been previously instructed in the protocol, when one or more of the children falter on a word, their teacher prompts them to stop to talk directly to one another, facilitating turn taking and questioning behaviors: "Oops, you guys read that word in a couple of different ways. Tommy said it was *lost* and Alvin said *losed*. Which one is it? Tommy, what made you say lost?" Tommy then points out the 't' and explains what sound it makes. "James, what do you think?" James then explains that he agrees with Tommy—the 't' offers evidence the word is *lost* rather than *losed*, further explaining that the word would have to end in a 'd' if it were *losed* (as five-year-old ESL students, none of the boys are yet able to conclude that *losed* also presents usage problems). Their teacher continues, "OK, James, tell Tommy and Alvin why you think so." With her support of their discussion processes, the children handle the content independently, naturally making references to picture and phonics cues as they figure out each problem word independently.

Young children at this stage are learning as much about how to be independent members of a classroom community and participants of small groups as they are about how texts work, and patterns of instruction will bear this out.

On the other hand, adolescents socialized into a peer culture of "dissin" or insulting one another need to be taught ground rules for civil discourse. "Laurent, you can't call Jin a liar. You can say you disagree, or ask why he said what he did. But you can't call him a liar." Or, "When you gasp and roll your eyes every time someone has a question, that discourages people from wanting to share their ideas and prevents everyone from learning. That's intimidating behavior, and takes away others' opportunity to learn. You don't have the right to take away anyone's opportunity to learn."

Once familiar with the Unison Reading protocol, middle school children can be quite adept at facilitating their own group processes. However, older children who have been used to highly teacher-directed instruction will need to learn how to act responsibly in a Unison Reading group. Social and communicative competencies become key factors in supporting independence, critical engagement, and competence in reading.

Instructional Accounting: Learning Standards as Reference Points

In addition to providing children with experiences that are engaging and autonomy supporting, the Unison Reading program also holds children responsible for meeting learning goals that are sanctioned by society. The Unison Reading program utilizes the Common Core Standards as tools for teaching and learning.

Progressive child-centered instructional approaches have often been criticized for failing to ensure that all children meet normative social standards and high learning standards (Olson, 2003). The tendency for these approaches to privilege students' self-oriented interests, it has been said, works against accountability to high learning standards (see Delpit, 1986; Hemphill & Snow, 1996). The explicit use of standards to guide instruction is a distinctive feature of Unison Reading. The Unison Reading method relies on teachers to exploit instructional opportunities as they arise in real time. Doing so effectively depends on teachers' knowledge of the standards, in order to choose those opportunities that will maximize students' learning. Unison Reading brings the locus of responsibility back into the hands of classroom teachers, rather than relying on commercial curriculums to deliver standards through a linear map of concepts to be dispensed and mastered.

Standards are a contract for both teacher and student. For students, they are a commitment from the school community that they will be provided opportunities to learn specific things. They are also an outline of the particular things that children must take responsibility for learning and what they must do to meet expectations. For teachers, standards outline professional responsibilities in the form of a full description of what children are expected to successfully do or understand, and so provide a reference to help map out the course for instruction. Every teacher and child in elementary and middle school should have access to the content of the standards documents. There should be no mystery to any student about what it is that he or she is supposed to have had the chance to learn. Standards are opportunity tools.

The Unison Reading program employs a system called *instructional accounting* to document how lessons align with formal standards. For some, the word "accountability" may conjure up an image of administrative surveillance—administrative record-keeping procedures and systematic observations designed to enforce compliance to a schedule of prescribed lessons. *Instructional accounting* is an entirely different paradigm, based on the principles of student and teacher autonomy and responsibility. Children need autonomy to make choices in their learning, and teachers need autonomy in using expertise and making decisions about what instruction their students need. But both teachers and students have the responsibility to meet particular obligations associated with their respective roles. For example, children must do particular tasks outlined in the standards (such as make connections, evaluate writing strategies, and summarize information, among others), and teachers must provide instruction and learning opportunities sufficient for students to successfully achieve these accomplishments. But if children have the autonomy to follow their curiosities, and teachers aren't expected to follow a prescribed sequence of lessons, how can we be sure that the standards are covered?

The "Standards Checklist" is the tool we use to keep track of the whole-class lessons that mark a trail of learning that aligns with official standards. (See Figure 2.8 for an example of a Standards Checklist from fourth-grade teachers' Ariel Ricciardi and Jaime Disken's combined general education/special education classroom.) It is comprised of formal standards incorporated into a spreadsheet-style format. At the time this book was written, New York City schools used the New Performance Standards (National Center on Education and the Economy and the University of Pittsburgh, 1997). The Genre Practice model, of which Unison Reading is a component, employs the Common Core State Standards, a comprehensive set of expectations for what American school children should learn in school in order to succeed after school (see Appendix B for the Genre Practice Reading and Speaking and Listening Standards Checklist for Fourth Grade as an example of the documents commonly used in every grade as a tool for the instructional inventory process). In the left column of the checklist are listed developmental indicators for reading. Dates in the spaces in the right-hand columns indicate when corresponding content was taught in large-group reading lessons. (Note: the checklist featured in Figure 2.8 lists indicators from the New Performance Standards, used prior to fall 2010 when the Common Core Standards were implemented.)

"Grass roots lessons": Standards-aligned instruction for the whole class

Teachers produce their own lesson content that, for the most part, recounts situations they have observed of their students demonstrating competencies that align with those delineated in the standards. Teachers refer back to the records they have taken in Unison Reading lessons and one-on-one reading conferences to select scenarios that illustrate what are deemed to be the most timely lessons (skills or strategies that most students would benefit from learning or those mandated in the standards that have not yet been addressed formally through group lessons). I call these "grass roots" lessons

Figure 2.8	Sample Standards Checklist, Ariel Ricciardi and Jaime Disken's Fourth-Grade Classroom

Reading: Comprehending informational materials (E1c)

Restates or summarizes information	11/10 11/16			
Relates new information to prior knowledge and experience	9/15 9/22			
Extends ideas	9/24			
Makes connections to related topics or information	9/24			

Reading: Read aloud fluently (E1d)

The student reads aloud accurately (in the range of 85–90%), familiar material of the quality and complexity illustrated in the sample reading list, and in a way that makes meaning clear to listeners by: Self-correcting when subsequent reading indicates an earlier miscue	10/5 10/29			
Using a range of cueing systems, e.g., phonics and context clues, to determine pronunciation and meanings	9/29 10/19 10/21			
Reading with a rhythm, flow, and meter that sounds like everyday speech (pp. 35–36)	9/9			

Source: Adapted from Board of Education of the City of New York (1997).

because they are harvested from teachers' face-to-face interactions and observations of their students' accomplishments.

Ariel explains how her work in Unison Reading informs the way she plans standards-based, large-group instruction:

During Unison Reading, I'm constantly thinking, OK, what's happening here in my group? And what I noticed that day and that would be the most beneficial for students to learn the next day. What do they need right now to make them more successful readers? I think about the four [domains] of reading from the [Unison Reading] Record and look at Unison Reading Records and notice the breaches [that students made] and what instructional points will benefit all students in their Unison Reading groups and in their independent reading. I plan lessons directly around the students' needs. Typically the lesson comes from something that has happened in a Unison Reading group or in an individual conference with students. Being knowledgeable about the standards and being diligent about keeping track of the lessons you've already taught into gives you a better sense of what you haven't taught.

> In addition to your knowledge of your students and what's happening daily in your classroom, you also have to be knowledgeable about the grade-level expectations. Using the Standards Checklist is a way that you check in. It holds the teacher accountable. This curriculum is based on accountability. Our students are always holding themselves accountable. The Standards Checklist holds the teacher accountable. It's like your own bookkeeping system. You're using all of the knowledge and experience you have from your students and checking in to see that that knowledge is also meeting the expectations of the grade. The real purpose of it is that we're giving the students what they need to succeed and move forward.

Every time Ariel teaches a reading lesson to the whole class, she logs the date into the Standards Checklist on the row corresponding to the Standards Indicator that best describes the content of the lesson. All teachers maintain a balanced focus by following a general guideline of devoting at least one lesson a week to each reading domain. With this flexibility, teachers have latitude to concentrate a series of lessons on a single area of focus if necessary, before returning to the lesson agenda. (See Figure 2.9 for a sample weekly lesson agenda.) This system is a way for lessons to be generated through teacher expertise and first-hand knowledge of students' strengths and needs, while also insuring that lessons align with the formal learning standards of the local education agency (city or state standards, for example).

Figure 2.9 Weekly Lesson Agenda

Monday	Tuesday	Wednesday	Thursday	Friday
Social Processes	Genre	Comprehension	Decoding/Strategic Processing	Optional/Catch up

Standards-Aligned Instruction Within Unison Reading Groups

It is possible to make judgments about the quality of learning experiences provided in Unison Reading sessions by cross-referencing instructional content against high-quality learning standards. Since children's points of confusion and curiosity become the focus of attention during Unison Reading, discussion naturally gives rise to instructional opportunities that relate to developmentally predictable points of concern. And since the content of high-quality standards mirror the typical literacy developmental trajectory instruction and standards should closely align.

To crosscheck instructional content against standards, simply list the instructional points generated in the Instructional Inventory section of the Unison Reading Analysis form (or refer directly to the form itself). In serial order, identify the comparable skill or competency found in any standards document used by your local educational agency. Record the standard by number and/or language descriptor.

This process is illustrated in Figure 2.10, where the content of the Instructional Inventory section of a Unison Reading Analysis from a narrative text read by students of third-grade teacher, Shara Miller, is presented in column A. Adjacent to each instructional point, listed in Column B, is the corresponding indicator from the reading portion of the Common Core Standards, the standards used in the Genre Practice model. This process, from a nonfiction text read by Shara's students, is illustrated in Figure 2.11. Shara comments on the process of crosschecking instructional points with the Common Core Standards,

I am amazed at how many of the standards are actually being met through the teaching points that come out of the dialog in Unison Reading. The speaking and listening standards are met every day through Unison Reading, whereas in other formats of teaching, like guided reading, you don't really focus on that part of the standards. In a transmission kind of curriculum, they're not getting that opportunity to respond to each other. That's not usually what you focus on when you teach reading.

Crosschecking instructional data against formal standards is enlightening. It provides evidence that organic conversations based on children's natural curiosities give rise to legitimate learning opportunities that meet the criteria of high-quality standards-based instruction; and can shed light on ways in which conversations might be more productively facilitated. But the process is also time consuming. Crosschecking records is an exercise in heightened awareness suitable for occasional professional development, but inappropriate as an expectation for routine recordkeeping.

Figure 2.10   Standards-Referenced Instructional Inventory: Fiction Text

Instructional Point	Standards Indicator
Text form (fictional story vs. fable), genre features, and expectations for reading	**RL5:** Refer to parts of stories, dramas, and poems when writing or speaking about a text, using terms such as chapter, scene, and stanza, describe how each successive part builds on earlier sections. **S1c:** Ask questions to check understanding of information presented, stay on topic, and link their comments to the remarks of others. **S1d:** Explain their own ideas and understanding in light of the discussion.
Using context clues/reading on to figure out a word and its meaning	**RF3d:** Read grade-appropriate irregularly spelled words **RF4c:** Use context to confirm or self-correct word recognition and understanding, rereading as necessary
Reader's opinion; responding to a text	**RL6:** Distinguish their own point of view from that of the narrator or those of the characters.
Summarize and evaluate text	**RL1:** Ask and answer questions to demonstrate understanding of a text, referring explicitly to the text as the basis for the answers. **S1d:** Explain their own ideas and understanding in light of the discussion.
Infer, draw conclusions about characters	**RL3:** Describe characters in a story (their traits, motivations, or feelings) and explain how their actions contribute to the sequence of events. **RL6:** Distinguish their own point of view from that of the narrator or those of the characters.
Rereading for meaning	**RF4c:** Use context to confirm or self-correct word recognition and understanding, rereading as necessary.

| Figure 2.11 | Standards-Referenced Instructional Inventory: Nonfiction Text |

Instructional Point	Standards Indicator
Text form (genre features and purpose	**RI2:** Determine the main idea of a text; recount the key details and explain how they support the main idea.
	RI5: Use text features and search tools (key words, sidebars, hyperlinks) to locate information relevant to a given topic efficiently.
	RI7: Use information gained from illustrations (maps, photographs) and the words in a text to demonstrate understanding of the text (where, when, why, and how key events occur).
Cross-checking	**RF3c:** Decode multisyllable words.
Rereading for meaning	**RF4c:** Use context to confirm or self-correct word recognition and understanding, rereading as necessary.
Inferring using context clues	**RI7:** Use information gained from illustrations (maps, photographs) and the words in a text to demonstrate understanding of the text (where, when, why, and how key events occur).
Unison Reading rules: Stopping when confused	**S1b:** Follow agreed-upon rules for discussions (gaining the floor in respectful ways, listening to others with care, speaking one at a time about the topics and texts under discussion).
	S1c: Ask questions to check understanding of information presented, stay on topic, and link their comments to the remarks of others.
Using prior knowledge to understand new vocabulary	**S1a:** Come to discussions prepared, having read or studied required material; explicitly draw on that preparation and other information known about the topic to explore ideas under discussion.
	RI4: Determine the meaning of general academic and domain-specific words and phrases in a text relevant to a Grade 3 topic or subject area.
Rereading for meaning	**RF4c:** Use context to confirm or self-correct word recognition and understanding, rereading as necessary.

SUMMARIZING PROCEDURES FOR IMPLEMENTATION

This chapter has presented a comprehensive description of how to implement Unison Reading at the classroom level. Once you have run a few Unison Reading groups in your classroom, and you feel like you have a foundation of expertise to build upon, begin plans for classroom implementation. I suggest you enlist the support of a few colleagues who are also willing to try Unison Reading along with you so that you will have a network of support and can share your experiences and strategies for success. Here are a set of procedures to follow:

1. Form a professional development group with other teachers and plan to meet periodically to share concerns and insights about Unison Reading. Before you begin the program, meet with your group to discuss your plan.

2. Assess your students using your school's system of leveling for reading or the measures listed earlier in this chapter. Rank your students on the Instructional Priority List in order of highest to lowest level of need.

3. The week prior to beginning Unison Reading, collect a wide supply of texts that children can choose from. Ask the children to help collect short texts that they think their classmates might be interested in reading.

4. Introduce students to the program by explaining the schedule, the role, and responsibilities of group leaders, and the system you have developed for giving them the opportunity to select texts.

5. Establish a system for rotating group leaders and share that system with students.

6. Meet with the first group of leaders to discuss text collecting. Bring a few samples of texts you think students might like to read as samples. Initially some students will rely on you to help them select texts.

7. Post or display texts, and invite the students to sign up for texts of their choice.

8. On Monday of the week you begin the Unison Reading program, plan to run only groups that meet with you. Begin the cycle of independent groups the following week when children have experience with the method.

9. On Monday of the week you begin the program, pull your first group, then your second. Remember to use the Unison Reading Record to take notes. While it might seem overwhelming at first, the process of note taking will remind you to let children in the group do most of the talking. It's important to establish norms for the group process that reinforce the idea that everyone should participate on an equal footing. If children look to you for permission to talk, teach them not to.

10. After the session, make sure to debrief with students in the group about the experience. Help them consider their peers' reactions to the texts selected in order to begin to develop the ability to critique a text and weigh its merits by assuming the perspectives of others.

11. Once all students in the class have had an opportunity to participate in Unison Reading, gather the whole class to debrief the experience as a large group. This will be a good opportunity for you to hear and respond to students' questions and criticisms.

12. Meet with your professional development group to share your experiences and questions. Use the Unison Reading Rubric (see Appendix A) as a reference to make judgments on the quality of your groups. The Rubric provides a list of quality indicators to help you assess Group Processes, Recordkeeping and Classroom Procedures, and Organization.

■ CONCLUSION: THE PARADOX OF RULES

This chapter provided a system of routines and procedures to assist you in implementing Unison Reading classroomwide. As you have observed, successful implementation depends on adherence to a specific set of rules that are designed to support student autonomy and agency. And in case you are struck by the irony of the strict specifications on one hand and the goal of student independence and agency on the other, I'll conclude this chapter with a word about rules. You can think of the rules of Unison Reading as having a similar function to black letter law. Just as the Civil Code protects basic freedoms in a democracy, rules in the classroom ensure consistent opportunities for children to exercise responsibility and agency in their learning. In traditional classrooms where teachers have central authority, rules tend to support the exercise of that authority. Rules can be simple: sit at your desk, don't talk, and do what I say. In classrooms where children are expected to assume substantial responsibility and authority, the system of rules needs to be strong enough to support the distribution of authority so that 25 or more individuals can enjoy the privilege of autonomy. When such a degree of responsibility is handed over to students, rules provide boundaries that contain activity, prevent chaos, guarantee the provision of instruction, and free the teacher from the need to intervene in every trivial matter. The Unison Reading program is essentially an organized system of rules that guarantees children the freedoms and opportunities necessary for them to take responsibility for their own learning. Eujin Jaela Kim (Jaela), the Grade 4–8 ESL teacher at the Jacob Riis School, comments on the positive impact the Unison Reading system has had on her students' level of independence:

I feel like I don't even have to be in my room anymore. It's like a student-run operation. One time I came to the classroom and I told my kids I had a meeting during the text sign-up and they said, "No Ms. Kim, we know what to do." I see this independence happening in all classrooms. As an ESL teacher, I step into CTT classrooms, 12 to 1 classrooms, middle school reading classrooms, and kids are working independently.

I think before when I stepped into reading in any given room I could always anticipate where it was going to go and what product you were going to get at the end. If the students didn't get to that end point, they would pass or fail. But now when I step into these different classrooms, you can't anticipate what's going to happen. It's almost like an adventure. It's almost like a tree—you never know where a new branch is going to sprout or what direction it might go. You never know where things are going to go or what the kids are going to say. It's not only enlightening for the children, but also for the teacher. I think that it was difficult to learn how to "teach on your feet," but Unison Reading has been a real awakening of the teacher inside me.

3

Distinctions
and Differences

How Unison Reading Breaks the Mold

By now you probably recognize that Unison Reading is substantively different from conventional reading practices and creates wholesome spaces for you and your students to learn and grow. Unison Reading is not just an innovative instructional approach; it's a movement to dislodge ancient pedagogical traditions that view teaching as telling and learning as imitating. If you've begun using Unison Reading in your classroom, you have probably encountered resistance that stems from centuries of established traditions of didactic, teacher-directed pedagogy that are deeply ingrained in our schools. You know that what you've been able to accomplish with your students during your Unison Reading groups is good. The question you might be asking is: how do I keep the goodness going? It's a tall order. Unison Reading is an approach, to be sure. But the first time you faced resistance to this new approach—from parents, administrators, or the children themselves—you experienced Unison Reading as a political movement.

If you're committed to the values that Unison Reading embodies, you've joined ranks with other teachers in the Genre Practice school reform community. Like us, you welcome the access to more knowledge as power to support your practice. This chapter is written to provide you with the critical knowledge you need to proceed with confidence. I begin with an examination of the overarching raison d'etre for Unison Reading and other conventional reading instruction models and traditions in order to address the questions:

- What broader aims does reading education serve within each paradigm?
- What theories inform practice?

This chapter discusses in more depth the principles of Unison Reading that were introduced in Chapters 1 and 2, and concludes with a comparative description of widely used reading instructional models and Unison Reading.

I want to reiterate that the Unison Reading approach rejects the traditional definition of reading as a process that happens solely inside a person's head. Rather, reading is also a cultural practice that relies on coordinated participation between people involved in conventionalized routines. I am also asserting that conventional reading instruction practices, based on *in-the-head* epistemologies, have created firmly established institutional traditions that in many respects have limited rather than supported literacy development in many children. The renowned cultural anthropologist, Ruth Benedict (1934) said, "Tradition is as neurotic as any patient; its overgrown fear of deviation from its fortuitous standards conforms to all the usual definitions of the psychopathetic" (p. 273). This chapter lays out some of the basic philosophical principles of reading explores practices that align with contemporary thinking on literacy and learning. Equipped with these insights, you will gain confidence in breaking with some of the more unhelpful traditions of reading instruction and gain confidence in your ability to implement Unison Reading.

THE AIMS OF READING ∎

Traditionally, reading programs identify the mastery of cognitive processes associated with proficient reading as the primary goal of instruction. Proficient readers decode fluently. They can summarize, infer, visualize, make connections, synthesize, and so forth. Instruction is designed to provide teachers with a method to direct students through sequentially arranged activities to help them independently master these competencies. Because the goal of reading instruction is for the student to master increasingly complex texts and to advance in reading level, the entirety of the reading curriculum is organized around assessing, grouping, and teaching children based on reading level. Thus, instruction is typically designed to guide students through sequentially arranged activities to help them independently master discrete skills and competencies associated with increasingly complex levels of text difficulty. Teaching consists essentially of facilitating the movement of children through sequentially ordered text levels. The metaphor could be that of an assembly line along which students progressively receive more skills and strategies to master more complex texts. In the interests of efficiency, children are organized by level to receive appropriately leveled instruction. To be sure, some children move from one level to another. But more typically, reading groups are like segregated neighborhoods. Some children, on occasion, move to a new location, but most children remain in the same neighborhood on an indefinite basis. While such "stability" might be comforting for some children who are already motivated by reading and feel some level of competence, it can induce boredom in others.

In instances when children aren't able to keep pace with the normal "assembly line" pace of instruction, it is assumed that the locus of difficulty rests within the individual child. Typically, children who show significant delays in literacy development are taken "off line" and provided with remediation in the form of special interventions designed to reinforce skills that appear weak or lacking—programs that in some cases add substantial additional costs to school budgets.

Unison Reading operates from a different system of logic, that assuming in cases where children experience difficulty reading texts at hand that the locus of difficulty is largely situational, as opposed to intrapersonal, and that adjustments to group or interpersonal processes are necessary to support individual ineptitudes. Though we expect children to be able to apply useful cognitive strategies appropriately while reading independently, and while we expect children will become more skillful as they mature as readers, these competencies are understood to materialize from classroom practices that satisfy children's personal goals that hold meaning and purpose. Reading, like language, is a means through which children learn to interpret and regulate their culture (Bruner, 1983). The Unison Reading approach strives toward broader aims than the mere acquisition of skills. Beyond the mere mastery of cognitive skills, the Unison Reading curriculum aims toward Deweyian-inspired, democratically oriented ideals of progressive education summarized below:

- maximize the interests that are shared in the classroom and encourage their variety,
- support the free interplay of associations amongst members of the group,
- support equal opportunities for all children in the group to participate with one another, and
- support a means by which understandings and experiences can be shared.

The Unison Reading approach seeks to expose each child to a multiplicity of group experiences so as to broaden their perspectives and opportunities to learn. By the end of the year, the child who has participated in a Unison Reading program will have participated in 30–40 different groups around 30–40 different texts, better achieving the expectations of a reading program that serves the democratic purposes of education.

■ GROUP READING INSTRUCTION: TRADITIONS AND CONVENTIONS

In order to underscore what makes Unison Reading distinctive as a method of group reading instruction, I will briefly survey existing methods of reading instruction. Conventional reading methods operate from the assumption that reading involves making meaning from text, and that decoding is central to that process. What the field has disagreed about, sometimes with vehemence, is the question of which end of the continuum should be emphasized through instruction, spawning what is commonly referred to as the *Reading Wars*. On one end of the continuum, skills instruction focuses on decoding and letter-sound relationships; and on the other end of the continuum, instruction focuses on meaning making through application of comprehension strategies. Instructional practices evolved in alignment with points on the continuum.

My own childhood reading experiences were typical of what was once a widespread practice called Round Robin reading. Children, once they showed signs of being "ready" for instruction, were grouped by ability, usually in low, medium, and high groups, and met several times a week with the teacher. Sitting in a circle, the children in each group took turns reading paragraphs aloud while the teacher listened. It was primarily the teacher's responsibility to monitor and reinforce oral reading accuracy and to intervene to help the child to correct errors.

While others were reading, I learned to skip ahead to the point in the text I would be asked to read and silently practiced. When it was my turn to read, with my heart racing, I read each word of the excruciating paragraph aloud as best I could. I was never told what the teacher was listening for, so I just tried my best not to make mistakes. Like most children, for me, reading in these situations was a performance, and I never cared much about what I read. The books were boring readers organized into a seemingly endless sequence of stories (contrived to align with increasing readability level). I never made it to the end of any of my readers. We were grouped by ability. I wasn't in the highest group, but I wasn't in the lowest either. And, being a self-conscious child, I was glad for that.

The implicit emphasis on reading as a performance, the focus on decoding accuracy and fluency, and the neglect of comprehension are the primary reasons that Round Robin reading is no longer advocated. Nonetheless, it is a custom that continues to persist. So deeply engrained in school culture is the practice of Round Robin reading that teachers who lack training in alternative methods fall back on the age-old practice of grouping children by ability and having them take turns reading aloud.

With advances in brain science, we now know that there are two primary routes to reading in the brain—the letter-to-sound route or the lexicosemantic route (Dehaene, 2009). The Reading Wars have subsided somewhat in response to a call to integrate and balance instruction by emphasizing both meaning and phonics skills, as both are required in the act of reading. Reading practices have evolved to attend to the need for instruction that balances an emphasis on skills and meaning.

The following are examples of just a few such approaches:

• *Transactional strategies instruction* "involves direct explanations and teacher modeling of strategies, followed by guided practice of strategies . . . [and] teacher assistance is provided on an as-needed basis. There are lively interpretive discussions of text as [and] there are no restrictions on the order of strategies execution or when the particular members of the group can participate" (Pressley, 2000, p. 555).

• *Reciprocal teaching* (Palinscar & Brown, 1984) is another model that emphasizes instruction of key cognitive strategies in the context of reading authentic texts. A protocol for scaffolding is provided by the teacher to hand over responsibility to children for predicting, clarifying, summarizing, and questioning in the context of reading.

• *The gradual release of responsibility* model (Pearson & Gallagher, 1983) begins with the teacher explaining and modeling, moving to guided practice in which children assume more responsibility, toward independent practice with feedback from the teacher, to the application of the newly learned strategy during independent reading.

Guided Reading and the Gradual Release Model

The Gradual Release of Responsibility model of reading instruction has become widespread in schools. This approach evolved under the influence of constructivism in learning psychology when the field of reading had begun to acknowledge that children come to school already knowing something about reading and develop new understanding through active involvement in reading activities in which they are expected to assume increasing responsibility for reading independently. The concept of teaching was now defined by the principles of acquisition in which the expert/teacher gradually releases responsibility for reading to the novice/student. The reading program was expanded and reconfigured to incorporate a fuller range of reading formats along the continuum of responsibility. The gradual release model of instruction unfolds along three points, beginning with the teacher assuming responsibility for teaching a skill or strategy through modeling and describing behavior, followed by joint responsibility for practicing the skill or strategy by the students and teacher together, ending with children's independent practice of the skill or strategy with the teacher's feedback and assistance as needed (Gambrell, Malloy, & Mazzoni, 2007; Holdaway, 1979).

Within the Gradual Release approach, several instructional formats provide opportunities for children and teachers to practice the activity along the responsibility continuum, as depicted below (see also Figure 3.1).

Literature Groups and Literature Circles

With the recognition that students benefit from opportunities to independently engage in discussions about their reading, practices known as Literature Groups (Peterson & Eeds, 1990) or Literature Circles (Daniels, 2002) have become widespread. These are

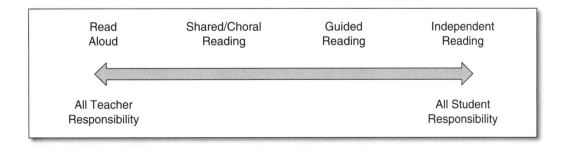

| Figure 3.1 | Distribution of Responsibility for Reading |

- *Read Aloud.* The teacher reads and the children listen. The text is typically only seen by the teacher, and he assumes all responsibility for decoding, freeing the child to focus on meaning. Visual cues are not a mediating factor in the child's reading experience.

- *Shared Reading.* The teacher leads the children in a shared reading experience in which the text is seen by all. Visual information is now a mediating factor. The teacher assumes most of the responsibility for decoding through an integrated process of attending to syntactic (structure/grammar), semantic (meaning), and visual (graphic/phonemic) language cues, while inviting children to participate in the process by reading along or chorally reading. Shared Reading is a context for large-group instruction through opportunities to demonstrate and explain desired reading behaviors.

- *Guided Reading.* Children are guided through the oral reading of a text in a situation that is highly scaffolded by the teacher who offers instruction relating to text features and ideas that are anticipated to create challenges for students. Instructional points are often preplanned based on the teacher's knowledge of students' reading level in relation to text difficulty. Before reading, the teacher involves children in what is known as a *picture walk* to think about what the story might be about. Within the context of guided reading lessons, children assume responsibility for independent reading under the watchful eye of the teacher. During the Guided Reading format the teacher facilitates and assists, letting children know when to begin reading and where to stop on the page. The children read simultaneously, and as they do so, the teacher monitors each individual child's reading process. During reading, she might stop periodically and prompt consideration about the way the words and pictures played a part in the reading process. Typical of most Guided Reading formats, children are grouped by common need or level. Most Guided Reading formats also involve some element of formal instruction—objective driven and preplanned—to address children's needs. Short lessons are often provided at the conclusion of the session (Fountas & Pinnell, 1996). Compared to Round Robin reading, where each child in a small group gave an independent reading performance in serial order, Guided Reading is now a matter of every member of a small group of children simultaneously engaged in an act of independently reading the same text.

- *Independent Reading* opportunities give children full responsibility to practice reading on their own, independently. It is the centerpiece of the Reading Workshop curriculum in most elementary classrooms because it presumably gives children time to integrate their reading skills and practice reading. It also gives teachers a context in which to assess children's oral reading on an individual basis.

organized to provide children opportunities to discuss previously read literature and emphasize the transactional or interpretive dimensions of the reading experience. The meanings children make of their reading become the focus of discussion. Children typically take responsibility for certain roles in the group that help provoke particular modes of thinking.

In spite of contributions such as these balanced, integrated solutions to the skills versus comprehension polemic, reading time in the average classroom today still bear a striking resemblance to reading time in the typical classroom, circa 1965, when the Reading Wars escalated. That is, the culture of reading instruction in classrooms has not changed enough to keep pace with new insights from learning theory, which emphasizes greater student responsibility, agency, and autonomy in learning. For the most part, children still work in small, ability- or level-based groups under the supervision of teachers who direct the reading activity. And whether situations call for children to focus on this strategy or that, reading programs continue to emphasize a relatively stable set of domains of reading conceptualized by the field of general psychology and remain focused on intramental cognitive processes, whether they be perceptual, linguistic, or meaning based.

While conventional reading practices emphasize a balance between skills and meaning instruction, they still target individual cognitive processes and neglect social interaction as a primary medium of new learning. Unison Reading operationalizes the social dimension of reading.

REDEFINING READING INSTRUCTION: UNISON READING AS A NEW SPACE FOR LEARNING

So where does Unison Reading fit within the range of reading instruction approaches? Unison Reading creates a new space for reading development that harnesses children's relationships and interactions with one another as a potent source of new learning. With its emphasis on student responsibility and the learning potential of social interactions, Unison Reading assigns new roles to teachers and students. Where both Round Robin and Guided Reading traditions invest the teacher with responsibility to plan and conduct lessons, Unison Reading transfers responsibility to determine the course of learning onto the children themselves. Children plan what to read, decide which text features to attend to and which ideas to discuss, and facilitate group discussion. While children have responsibility to actually read during Guided Reading lessons, the teacher is responsible for facilitating the group process, stopping and starting the group, asking questions, providing instruction, and soliciting student input. In Unison Reading, each child, in addition to being responsible for his independent reading process, is also responsible to the group's collective reading process by staying in sync and stopping to discuss points of confusion or interest. The locus of control over the direction of learning, which was once solely the teacher's, is now redistributed to the children. In fact, the ultimate goal for Unison Reading is to support children in conducting their own groups and resolving their questions independently of the teacher.

Differences and distinctions between Guided Reading and Unison Reading are detailed by Tara Clark, a K/1 teacher, in Figure 3.2.

Unison Reading redefines group reading instruction and acknowledges that the act of reading is first and foremost a social experience. The skills traditionally associated with reading—phonics and phonemic awareness, vocabulary knowledge, fluency, and comprehension—are subsumed within an overarching concern for reading as a social process. Of course, these skills are deployed as they are needed in the context of reading any given text, but they are drawn upon to meet the needs of the reader depending on the demands of the social situation in which reading is being practiced.

Unison Reading draws from a view of psychology that helps explain the role that others play in the child's development. When reading is approached as a social practice—employed by people as means to accomplish goals—then the ways in which people interact with others as readers and writers become significant factors in literacy processes. The relationship that the child has with the teacher, or expert, is of course significant. But also significant are the relationships with other children in the classroom. These relationships are a potentially rich source of social interaction and, as a consequence, new understandings that unfold through them. Participation with others in literacy situations that are meaningful and purposeful yields deeper understandings about how language works. Because relationships are such an important source of new learning, the Unison Reading method includes *social processes* as an important domain of reading and a critical concern for pedagogy. Children are taught to discuss and disagree, and to seize opportunities to do so.

Unison Reading shares similarities to other reading instruction approaches in that one teacher and a few children each have a copy of the same text and everyone reads it with attention to text features and meaning. But what may seem to be subtle differences on their face become more pronounced when the roots of theory of each approach are traced back their source. Whereas conventional reading practices are informed by

| Figure 3.2 | Comparison of Teacher and Student Responsibilities in Guided Reading and Unison Reading |

Guided Reading: Division of Responsibilities

Teacher Responsibilities	Student Responsibilities
• Level students • Create homogeneous groups based on level • Select books (at guided level with one or two new concepts) • Predetermine focus of instruction • Teach one skill or strategy per session • Read title (levels A–D) • Introduce book (activate prior knowledge) • Direct "picture walk" • Set reading pace • Assessment page: teacher checks for application of skill or strategy • Share out insight at the end of the book • Ask comprehension questions at the end of the book	• Participate as member of group organized by teacher • Read book chosen by teacher • Listen to teacher's book introduction • Participate in teacher-directed picture walk (respond to teacher's questions) • Repeat and remember new concepts and vocabulary • Read when the teacher says to read and stop when the teacher says to stop (follow teacher's pace) • Read quietly/silently by yourself when not in group • Read aloud when the teacher comes to assess • Apply strategies/skills taught independently or with teacher's help • Answer comprehension questions at conclusion of book

Unison Reading: Division of Responsibilities

Teacher Responsibilities	Student Responsibilities

• Set Unison Reading rules with group
• Facilitate group process
• Contribute insights as one of the "more knowledgeable other" members of the group
• Observe, take notes, and assess (Unison Reading Record)
• Use data for "grass roots" lesson planning (whole-class lessons during the reading block)
	• When group leader, choose text
	• Sign up for Unison Reading group
	• Acknowledge Unison Reading Rules:
	  ○ Read in unison
	  ○ Read so group members can hear
	  ○ Breach at points of confusion
	  ○ Stop the group to share an insight, new understanding, or to help the group resolve a problem
	  ○ Listen and respond to other members
	  ○ Meet in Unison Reading group with and without teacher, twice each week
	  ○ As group member, set goals and be accountable for meeting them
	  ○ Commit to the group and the process of learning to read

Source: Clark (2009).

general psychology, Unison Reading traces its roots to cultural psychology, a substantially different philosophical paradigm. Though individual cognitive processes are addressed, the Unison Reading method attends equally to interactions between and amongst members of the learning group, trusting that new insights will be acquired on what Vygotsky called the intermental plane, or "social plane," and then integrated into the intramental plane to become individual cognitive abilities. Higher-order thinking skills are born in social situations where literacy is used. Therefore, social processes and group dynamics are as significant to the cause of reading instruction as cognitive strategies instruction.

Rather than read merely for the sake of reading better by mastering cognitive demands, children are expected to read in order to accomplish broader personal and social goals, such as reading to participate in social groups, reading and talking about reading in order to practice civil discourse, reading to explore one's identity, reading as a means to be in relationships with others, and reading to acquire a greater sense of agency and autonomy in thought and action. To be sure, basic cognitive skills and strategies are critical to any of these abstract goals, and concrete goals having to do with word attack, invoking comprehension strategies, learning vocabulary, and monitoring, self-correcting and cross checking are all vitally important to the larger purposes of reading. When children are held accountable to their larger goals as readers, they master the competencies of reading.

The Unison Reading approach emphasizes the role of agency in learning as opposed to an emphasis on a curriculum focused on coverage of discrete skills and strategies. Debating whether instruction should emphasize meaning or skills misses the more salient point that the demands of the situation in which reading is used determines which domains deserve attention. Learning how to effectively make on-the-spot judgments about which strategies to deploy should be the focus of instruction. The opportunity to learn occurs when something appears in the crosshairs of a child's attention and throws everything a little off kilter—maybe a letter, maybe an idea. In the process of regrouping her mental schemes to regain a sense of order, she learns something. Lacking from the field of literacy is a coherent pedagogical approach that confers responsibility for learning on children, thereby enhancing agency as a critical factor in the learning process. Unison Reading addresses the disconnect between (1) what is known about the nature of learning and (2) the ways in which conventional schooling deprives children of opportunities to learn.

AN EXAMINATION OF UNISON READING PRINCIPLES

As introduced in Chapters 1 and 2, the basic method of Unison Reading rests on a foundation of important principles derived from key psychological and philosophical ideas. Having a deeper understanding of the logic that underlies the practice will give you confidence as you begin to experiment with the Unison Reading method.

Social and Communicative Competencies: Important Learning Factors

In addition to helping children learn to read fast, accurately, and with expression, and to comprehend what they read, Unison Reading also strives to teach children to be responsible members of a social group with social competencies that allow them to participate successfully in order to access new ideas and collaborate with others in achieving collective understanding. Where as conventional reading practices are mostly focused on the cognitive demands of reading, Unison Reading places an equal value on a concern for interactions between and amongst members of the group, with the understanding that these processes are the medium of new insights and understandings. Social processes and group dynamics are as significant to learning as cognitive strategies instruction. Therefore, in addition to emphasizing the cognitive demands of reading, Unison Reading also emphasizes the role of reading groups as a context for pursuing broader personal and social goals, such as: reading as a context to learn to successfully participate in social groups, reading and talking about reading in order to practice civil discourse, reading and talking about reading in the company of others as a means to explore one's identity, reading and talking about reading as a means to develop relationships with others, and reading in the company of others to acquire a greater sense of agency and autonomy in thought and action. Unison Reading rests on the logic that higher-order thinking skills such as those employed in literate thinking are the product of participation in social situations where literacy is used. When children are held accountable to these larger goals as readers, they also learn to master the basic competencies of reading.

Skills are developed in the context of practicing the conventionalized behaviors associated with the Unison Reading format. Though skills are deployed and discussed in the context of reading, the overarching goal of every Unison Reading session is functional appropriateness versus skill mastery. This pedagogical approach marks a departure from the more ubiquitous didactic approaches to classroom reading instruction in which teachers plan and execute lessons organized according to a hierarchy of skills that students are then expected to practice and master. Children have opportunities to attend extensively to the skills of reading within the Unison Reading context, as evidenced, for example, by the instructional inventories of the Unison Reading analyses featured in Chapter 1 (see Figures 1.6, 1.8, and 1.10).

The Unison Reading Format: A Medium for Student Agency

As opposed to the *traditional reading* lesson, the Unison Reading situation is organized around what is known as a *transactional format*. This term was coined by Jerome Bruner to describe routinized and familiar settings that facilitate comprehension on the part of the child in the process of language acquisition. According to Bruner, formats combine both speech and nonspeech elements in constrained situations that promote communicative effectiveness. Bruner (1983) writes

> In time and with increasing systematicity, formats are assembled into higher-order subroutines and in this sense can be conceived of as the modules from which more complex social interaction and discourse are constructed. In time and with increasingly abstractness, formats become like moveable feasts. (p. 121)

Competence arises as children take advantage of opportunities to use and perfect the highly formatted Unison Reading routines, and they expand as new routines are mastered. In this way, Unison Reading formats are like "moveable feasts." The ability to transfer what is learned in one context to another is enhanced by greater student agency and responsibility; that is, the skills learned in transactional formats are highly "detachable" (Bruner, 1983).

In much the same way that language interaction formats frame infant-caregiver language interactions and provide *Language Acquisition Support Systems* to help children master the uses of language (Bruner, 1983), Unison Reading routines provide children with a *Literacy Acquisition Support System* to help frame social interactions in such a way that help children master the routines and uses of a variety of texts. The Unison Reading experience takes place around formats that are specialized, scriptlike communicative routines that give children on-going opportunities to take part in conventionalized literacy interactions.

As children master the conventionalized behaviors of the Unison Reading protocol, they apply them to other contexts. With an emphasis on transactional participation within the context of the *format* as opposed to the traditional objective of mastering a sequence of skills, the child learns to manage their own agency and take on responsibility as participants in situations where reading is required. Through opportunities to choose which texts to read, establish reading goals, and set the terms for performing collaborative reading activities, Unison Reading allows children to assume responsibility for managing their forward momentum as persons who are able to use the skill of reading to meet the demands of an increasingly broad range of social situations.

Teacher as group facilitator

Because so much of the learning potential of the Unison Reading format involves the ability for children to pose questions and solve them, the primary role of the teacher during Unison Reading is that of facilitator who holds group members accountable to the group process. Unlike conventional reading instruction methods, in which the teacher is expected to execute a predetermined instructional plan, the entire potential of Unison Reading depends on the teacher's ability to follow into points of need that arise organically during the reading process. Pre-prescribed lesson plans are antithetical to the aims of Unison Reading and the expectation that children will develop the capacity to recognize and resolve their own questions and curiosities. Teachers intervene only when children signal a need.

Since so much learning within the group depends on relational factors—the things that happen along the relationship pathways between group members—Unison Reading involves teachers in facilitating and monitoring the group process. This doesn't need to be a scary new worry, but an invitation to use social skills that are already developed. You are probably relatively good at relationships. In order to have accomplished the many achievements necessary in becoming a teacher, you had to have demonstrated your competence in forming and sustaining relationships. And you use these skills continuously—to arbitrate playground conflicts or lunchroom quarrels. The Unison Reading method views interpersonal conflict as opportunities to learn and asks teachers to exercise their existing knowledge about relationships as they facilitate the interactions between children. If second-grader Liam is pouting because he thinks the group should begin reading a paragraph beyond the place suggested by Steven, both Liam and Steven have lost focus on the book: the former because he is frustrated, the latter because he is concerned that his friend is mad at him. In this instance, the teacher mediates by addressing Liam's need to regulate his emotions and use words to explain his frustration. She facilitates a discussion whereby the children decide a logical strategy to begin at the first point of confusion in fairness to the person whose confusion arose earliest in the text. These interactions provide an example of the centrality of socioemotional concerns to the pedagogical situation. Within a more conventional approach to instruction, they would be considered peripheral according to conventional reading instruction practices, as they do not fall within the categories of scientifically proven reading instruction practices. The teacher might be inclined to quickly mete out a solution in order to move on to more "substantive" concerns. In Unison Reading, we welcome these interactions as opportunities to teach into relational dynamics that are central to reading.

Together, in Unison: Why We Read Aloud in Synchrony

The words, "together, in unison," occupy a familiar place in my experience. As a child, they were the minister's invitation to our congregation to join together to actively participate in a spiritual experience. Even now reading or singing in unison with others puts me in a different place and brackets off the moment to allow me to notice the experience. We are wired to connect to others through voice and sound. Some innate need to be in communion with others has always expressed itself in human cultures, whether it be the practice of communal chanting of prelinguistic clans, pledges of allegiance, or reading passages of scripture.

In spite of the power of the voice, in most classrooms the voices of students are silenced. Schooling practices, particularly in the area of reading, have strictly limited opportunities for students to communicate with others. Several decades of research in the learning sciences have established that children learn best when they have opportunities to learn from others. Unison Reading capitalizes on the potential of oral language in the context of the reading curriculum. The Unison Reading rules help teachers *tame* the social space of the classroom so that children can use their voices as the primary medium of learning without too much clamor.

Reading aloud will initially seem a little strange to older children who have been socialized to silent reading. After all, silent reading is a school norm after second grade, when children learn to "subvocalize" (or vocalize in the mind only). Of course, silent reading eliminates noise, speeds up the reading process, and signals student independence. And while it is a useful technology for independent work, it is counterproductive to the form of group learning that makes Unison Reading powerful. If you are a teacher of older children, one challenge you might face is to help them become comfortable reading aloud. Knowing why reading aloud is beneficial will help you help your students become more willing to read aloud together.

One of the most eloquent testaments to the power of reading aloud comes from Verlyn Klinkenborg, who writes in the NY Times Editorial Observer (2009), " . . . one of the most basic tests of comprehension is to ask someone to read aloud from a book. It reveals far more than whether the reader understands the words. It reveals how far into the words—and the pattern of the words—the reader really sees."

The act of reading aloud in synchrony with others accomplishes five important objectives that are important for you and your students to understand:

1. *Instruction is immediate.* Synchronized oral reading lends a degree of immediacy to the process by involving all group members in the same experience where they are able to attend to exactly the same text features. When points of confusion arise, all eyes are literally on the same point, facilitating *follow in* and the phenomenon of the X-factor.

2. *Instruction is powerful.* Conventional reading methods specify that the teacher determines the point of instruction and ask children to follow in with their attention. In Unison Reading, the children themselves breach the reading process with their questions and confusions, dictating points of follow in to already established points of attention. Attention is coordinated with others in the group, all of whom are more attentive and responsive to instruction that is naturally targeted to established points of engagement.

3. *Instruction is efficient.* Synchronized reading eliminates the need for group participants to use procedural language to calibrate points of attention to the text for deliberation, facilitating the momentum of reading (comments such as, "stop," or "hold on," are sufficient to initiate follow in to the point where the breach occurs).

4. *Instruction is attuned to social instincts.* Reading in unison also lends itself to heightened intersubjective understanding—reading in unison involves everyone in a collective experience, facilitating intersubjective thinking. We can speculate about why this is so. It turns out that in the brains of people (and other animals) are what are known as "mirror neurons," brain cells that fire when one sees or hears another person do or say something and responds just as if it were his or her action (Rizzolatti & Craighere, 2004). If one member registers humor or shock at a particular point in the text, others in the group are hard-wired to experience the same emotion.

Achieving Social Understanding Through the *Breach*

The Unison Reading protocol asks children to breach the group when they have questions or contributions. This practice serves an important pedagogical function: it encourages children to become self-aware of their own reading process, to monitor their understanding, and to get help when they are confused. Stopping to attend to miscues or misunderstandings gives children the opportunity to experience a system of self-monitoring on the "social plane," whereby the reader is able to benefit from the insights of others. These insights can, over time, be internalized. Breaching is also a process that allows members of a group to achieve mutual understanding of a text.

The concept of the breach and its instructional protocol was inspired by the work of psychologist Kenneth Gergen and his theory of the relational conception of social understanding. Gergen (1990) explained that relationships between people are the primary locus of the development of new understanding, and intellectual development depends on human interchange. Literacy development, for example, can't be taken out of the context of the relationships in which literacy learning is situated. The nature of a relationship depends upon the mutual coordination of action between participants. As coordination of action progresses, a *relational nucleus* is formed. A relational nucleus is "a self-sustaining system of coordinated actions in which two or more persons are engaged" (Gergen, p. 585). The relational nucleus is a social accomplishment built and sustained through time. The relational nucleus offers a metaphor for the properties of the relationship between and the learner, teachers, and fellow students. The process of building a relationship depends on the capacity of participants in a situation to resolve conflict in order to maintain understanding. Gergen refers to this process as *adjudication*. As a judge adjudicates conflicts in the courtroom, so too do participants in a relationship adjudicate conflicts in understanding. The relational nucleus is an outcome of patterns of adjudication and the mutual coordination of actions between participants. The breach is a way of adjudicating issues that arise during the course of a collective reading of a text. Through the conversation that ensues after the breach, understanding is accomplished through the coordinated involvement of participants.

"Don't tolerate confusion!"

Most children, of any age, when they initially learn the Unison Reading protocol approach reading aloud mechanically, as if their intention was primarily to quickly decode. This is to be expected from a generation of children who have been raised on reading programs that emphasize reading speed and accuracy. Symptoms of such mechanical reading include substituting nonsense words or words that don't make sense when they come to words they don't know or reading over punctuation. They steadily grind a path through words on the page like a combine harvester plows through a field of corn. Somewhere along the way they were taught to make guesses for unknown words, but didn't learn that substitutions must make sense, sound right, and look right, in other words, that what they read should mean something (Clay, 2002). Some children have learned that reading is merely fast, accurate decoding and not a complex form of thinking. The process of thinking while reading and monitoring the achievement of meaning is something all readers need to master. Developing readers need to learn how to be engaged in the process of making sense in order to know when something does not make sense. This is a fact that applies equally to high-functioning and low-functioning readers alike. I've repeatedly seen a "lower" reader breach the group because she or he doesn't know a word's pronunciation or meaning. The "higher" reader, on a tacit hunch, will jump in to explain, but then realize suddenly that she or he cannot do so adequately. These moments, when the familiar becomes strange, and the child is pressed to solidify understanding through language, are vital learning opportunities for even the most proficient of readers.

Unison Reading emphasizes *in-process* sense making at the word and sentence level. Because each and every word is significant to the intended meaning of the text, unknown words are never glossed over. When someone in the group experiences confusion, all children take part in a process of its resolution. Through ongoing opportunities to be fully attentive to all features of a text, children learn to engage metacognitively and metalinguistically by participating in a collective reading process where these habits of mind are practiced.

Don't tolerate confusion is one of the most important principles that children are taught. In a typical Unison Reading session, children might stop at a half-dozen unknown words to decode them and discuss their meanings, and then reread the sentences in which they appeared to achieve the full meaning. This method rests on the assumption that the critical, engaged stance that children assume during Unison Reading becomes internalized in the child's independent reading process.

Children also need to learn to make judgment calls during the reading process. All readers come to those occasional words whose precise meaning or pronunciation cannot be immediately known. At that point, the reader needs to make a judgment call: is inference enough, or does comprehension hinge on full understanding? For example, we can usually get away with a best guess when we come to words that stand for place names or people and still preserve the overall meaning of the text since the meaning of the word is simply the thing the word represents. Specialized terms or words used to express particular meanings in the context of the surrounding sentence might require a little more thought, such as words that contain morphemes signaling salient clues about the relationship of the word to the overall meaning of the sentence or passage. While the child might not know the word, knowledge of the morpheme can trigger a line of reasoning that can lead to understanding the word (and sentence). The logic of meaning making in these instances is often quite involved, and children need to learn to persevere using whatever means available to achieve understanding. We often misleadingly emphasize that it is primarily the acquisition of skills, such as phonics knowledge or sight word vocabulary, that results in reading development. Actually, the attitudes and intentions that provoke the use of skills are just as important. But since dominant reading epistemologies neglect intentions and attitudes as central processes, they are often neglected in instruction. But unless we attend to attitudes and intentions, we reinforce the false impression that reading is the mechanical application of skills rather than the personal achievement of meaning. Persistence, perseverance and insight are as important as skills and are learned dispositions. *Don't tolerate confusion!* is a mantra heard in Unison Reading lessons at all levels to reinforce reading agency (see Figure 3.3 Posted Reminder: "Don't Tolerate Confusion!"). Unison Reading helps children learn *how* to make the kind of judgment calls in their reading that will help them independently read for understanding.

"A mistake can be an opportunity to make yourself smarter."

The Unison Reading method is premised on the idea that literacy competencies arise through opportunities to maximize cognitive dissonance. When we encounter confusion in reading a text, dissonance triggers the mind to accommodate and assimilate new insights. Unison Reading groups are organized so that points of dissonance are mediated as group members offer collective insights. Through social learning within the group children have opportunities to learn how to resolve dissonance by observing others.

Because Unison Reading is designed to exploit dissonance, and because there is a system of social interaction and support in place to resolve it, there is more tolerance for reading

Figure 3.3   Posted Reminder: "Don't Tolerate Confusion!"

miscues and confusion than is typically the case with conventional methods. Children are expected to breach the group at the point of confusion and admonished when they neglect to do so. The mindset that mistakes and miscues initiate learning opportunities counters conventional wisdom. For example, Block and Parris (2008) suggest that

> One mistake or a tiny fear that a student is going to make a mistake while reading activates his or her amygdala, the fear center of the brain. Either one is just as powerful, because both chemical changes lead to a biological neural connection that causes the student to perceive reading as a fearful experience . . . instruction should reduce the mistakes students make. (p. 122–123)

Perhaps it is not mistakes themselves that provoke fear or task avoidance. Rather, it is the child's orientation toward potentially negative situations that either contributes to competence or undermines it. Children who hold a theory about their own ability that is "fixed" or innate believe that mistakes are further evidence of their lack of competence; and children who have a "growth" or an "incremental" mindset about intelligence see competence as a result of effort and learning (Dweck, 2006). Children who hold a "growth" theory of intelligence embrace mistakes and challenges as opportunities to improve performance, while children who hold a "fixed" theory of intelligence learn to avoid challenging situations since failure and mistakes are evidence of inadequacy. Moreover, children's theories of intelligence are malleable; and the child who possesses a fixed mindset about intelligence can learn to adopt a growth theory of intelligence (Dweck, 2006). Instruction focused on helping children avoid mistakes may merely serve to enable children's maladaptive reading behaviors by reinforcing existing entity self-theories. The Unison Reading method creates a climate of collective support where risk taking and mistake making are viewed as welcome opportunities to learn. And perhaps because teachers and students assume an informal stance in their roles as participants in Unison Reading formats, the pressure of a traditional pedagogical situation is diminished. For example, teachers don't experience pressure to "train" students, and students aren't subjected to pressure to respond correctly. Unison Reading conversations exhibit the reciprocity of informal conversation in which language is a vehicle for inquiry, not a test of competence.

Rereading—When and Why

Though children are expected to decide for themselves at which point in the text to begin the rereading process after they close the breach, we encourage them to reread the complete sentence in which the breach occurred after it is closed. Rereading the complete sentence

- preserves sense at the sentence level,
- allows the child who made the breach to hear the way the words should sound when pronounced as they were intended by the author, and
- gives children an opportunity to regain passage-level cohesion after having stopped for discussion.

Rereading is particularly beneficial for children who speak non-standard varieties of English and children learning English in order to develop fluency and an ear for Standard English.

The X Factor: Instructional Opportunities Arise

Unison Reading employs an implicit form of pedagogy that revolves around genuine interactions as opposed to deliberate demonstrations or modeling offered in advance to then be imitated or practiced by students, the latter of which is characteristic of transmission modes of instruction. Pedagogical opportunities occur when children are faced with challenges in the context of authentic attempts to negotiate texts when they appeal to their teacher or group mates to intervene and *follow in* to the point of confusion through reciprocal conversation. The focus of instruction is indefinable until the moment arises at which point it is needed.

The "X Factor" is a term used to describe an elusive or indefinable quality. Within the context of Unison Reading, the X Factor refers to understanding that materializes through discussions that follow a breach. We don't know before we begin the reading process which points in the process will demand attention. Points of instruction are indefinable prior to the moment they arise. Unison Reading is governed by the X Factor principle: the aim of instruction always springs from the moment when readers themselves determine what the focus of instruction must be. Learning objectives are never predetermined or taken from external sources of authority (such as a lesson or unit objective from a commercial curriculum), and instruction never comes from a preprescribed plan, such is the case with traditional reading instruction methods.

The X Factor is something Dewey alluded to in his treatises on Progressive education. He explained that when teaching points are identified prior to the moment in which they are required,

> The external idea of the aim leads to a separation of means from end, while an end which grows up within an activity as plan for its direction is always both ends and means, the distinction being only one of convenience. Every divorce of end from means diminishes by that much the significance of the activity and tends to reduce it to a drudgery from which one would escape if he could. (Dewey, 1944, p. 106)

GLOSSARY: NOMOTHETIC

Relating to research methods that generalize findings about objective phenomena through large sample measures

The field of reading research and reading education has habitually ignored the X Factor; separating the ends from the means in programs of applied research, which are based on **nomothetic** measures and lead to one-size-fits-all methods.

Single strategy instruction is a recent example of this approach, in which the criteria of good reading is identified in terms of isolated behaviors, such as summarizing, questioning or predicting. Instruction is prescribed to help the student master those behaviors, one strategy at a time (see Block, Parris, & Whiteley, 2008; Keene & Zimmermann, 1997). Methods like these are not sensitive to the separation of ends and means, the outcome of which David Olson (2009a) cautions about: "The danger of enumerating criteria is that, too readily, they become the direct object of instruction rather than remaining, as they should be, specialized devices for advancing communication and understanding in particular domains" (p. 574).

When children are engaged in personally interesting text, when they are accountable to raising questions as they arise, when they are supported by members of their group, and when they feel safe enough to *mess up* in front of others, decoding errors and comprehension confusions materialize into a rich instructional dialog. Teachers, with their tacit knowledge of texts and informed understanding of their students, can predict where children will falter, and they know where to be vigilant to and intervene where the children may need support. The method proposed here for teaching into the focus of need is distinctive from teaching preassessed needs according to a formal instructional plan, which can interfere with children's agency and stifle the interpersonal processes that Unison Reading relies upon to support new learning.

This is not a call for laissez-faire teaching. In fact, you need to stay vigilant and attend to needs as they arise, teaching into them as you see fit. As the more experienced reader, you will notice plenty of teaching opportunities. But supporting agency and autonomy in students is a priority and your contributions should be made as an equal member of the group without dominating. As a member of the group, it is your prerogative to step in and ask questions of the group. But if you find you are dominating the conversation, it's important to step back and to let the children know that they have an equal responsibility to raise points for discussion. The children should eventually initiate the large proportion of "lessons," since this signals their increasing independence in reading critically.

You'll find that a substantial number of breaches will have to do with the technical features of texts—the structure of words, language, grammar, and punctuation. Be prepared for these instructional opportunities. Come to each group with a notepad, scrap paper, or white board so you can teach into points of confusion (spelling patterns, punctuation conventions, and so on). To be sure, children will fumble over letters and their sounds, words, ideas, the structure of texts, and concepts. Unison Reading provides a role for both teacher and student to let their needs come to the center of the group for discussion where those needs are allowed to be the objects of instruction. And because children hold one another accountable to resolving confusions and errors in their reading, it is expected that the group will provide a social medium in which undesirable reading behaviors are eliminated and generative ones established and secured.

Always mindful of time, we teachers are sometimes inclined to respond to children's confusions by giving them the answers so that they can be on their way. But confusion is where learning begins its potential. *Telling isn't helping* is a mantra in Unison Reading groups, and one that teachers do well to remember. When children encounter a word or idea they don't know, it can take a substantial number of turns in conversation to arrive at a conventional understanding. The X Factor has a pace all its own. A group of second graders in Anna-Lisa Corsi's classroom took 18 turns in conversation to arrive at a suitable understanding for the word *layered.* Just make sure, before they read on, that the breach is *closed* with a conventionally acceptable understanding.

The X Factor is a reminder that the situation determines what skills or strategies should be deployed to solve a problem. This pragmatic stance counters the neat and linear way many teachers were taught to teach reading. Third-grade teacher, Rachel Goren explains:

> I always knew that, as a good reader, I had to use all these strategies when I read. But I was always taught when you teach it to kids you can't combine them, that they were separate. They're not going to understand if you present too much at once. But Unison Reading has made me rethink everything that I've been taught. Unison Reading teaches kids to be real readers because they're doing all the strategies at the same time. For me it was very liberating, because I could see that they could do this. They were learning from it. They were *really* learning from it.

The typical Unison Reading session provides children with extensive explicit instruction. It's not uncommon for a group to work through one or two dozen instructional points in one session (recall that Tara's Unison Reading Record analysis in Figure 1.6 contained 16 instructional points and Lauren's in Figure 1.8 contained 19 instructional points). The sheer quantity of instructional points that receive explicit attention in a Unison Reading session far exceed the number of instructional points typically planned for in a traditional reading lesson.

Real Comprehension: Opening New Perspectives

Conventional conceptions of reading comprehension are based on the understanding that proficient readers are able to execute a range of mental functions to achieve deeper understanding of what they read (such as inferring, questioning, synthesizing, predicting). These functions are typically taught through exercises and activities that are designed to target them. The Unison Reading method redefines comprehension as a social accomplishment in which higher levels of mental functioning and understanding are made possible through the reader's ability to successfully participate in conventionalized means of communication. Through ongoing participation in situations in which particular texts are used, related forms of thinking and understanding develop. This pragmatic interpretation of comprehension, inspired by the language philosophy of Paul Grice (1989), recognizes that understanding depends not only on the reader's personal intentions but also on his or her facility with the conventions of the text at hand and the larger social situation in which it is begin used. Facilitating the child's ability to successfully participate in this *Gricean cycle,* as opposed to the emphasis of mastery of isolated cognitive functions, is the basis of comprehension instruction within the Unison Reading approach. Cognitive functioning develops to the extent that the child is able to master the conventions of the social situations in which texts are used.

As a competent social participant, the child is able to access and assimilate new ideas through cognitive operations such as inferring, questioning, predicting, or synthesizing, depending on the demands of the situation. Comprehension is the ability to control cognitive functioning in ways that best meet the demands of the situation. To emphasize the acquisition of cognitive skills in isolation and apart from the authentic situations in which they are used puts the cart before the horse. The Unison Reading method emphasizes the need for students to master conventionalized reading routines as a means to exercise and develop cognitive control. Expanded comprehension is impossible if children don't learn how to recognize when they don't understand or if they lack the empathetic capacity to relate to others as a means to achieve joint understanding of new ideas. Comprehension capacity, rather than the achievement of a sum of cognitive abilities, is the disposition to be open-minded and receptive to new ideas together with the ability to cooperate with others to achieve communal understanding.

Literacy is not only a process of accessing new ideas and expanding memory, but the process of raising awareness of the properties of language (Olson, 2009b). The method of Unison Reading expands the agenda of comprehension instruction to focus not only on the meanings that are derived from the reading experience, but the discursive abilities that are also achieved. Opportunities to take part in the routinized Unison Reading group experiences provide children with experiences to not only mine language for new ideas, but to master language as a means to facilitate discursive practice. The awareness not only of what language says, but how language works is an outcome of the Unison Reading experience.

But the rule of whole texts gives rise to an important opportunity for children to learn to evaluate the texts they read based on their tacit understanding of how language works.

The language philosopher, Paul Grice (1989), proposed several maxims that explain the pragmatic qualities of mature language. Speakers (and writers) more or less naturally observe these principles in cooperative interactions with others. And when something is stated (or written), the listener (or reader) makes assumptions about the meaning of the utterance based on these ground rules of communication and the contexts in which the utterance was made.

Grice's Conversational Maxims appear below.

Maxim of quantity: 1) Make your contribution as informative as is required (for the current purposes of the exchange); 2) Do not make your contribution more informative than is required

Maxim of quality: Try to make your contribution one that is true. 1) Do not say what you believe to be false; 2) do not say that for which you lack adequate evidence

Maxim of relation: Be relevant

Maxim of manner: Be perspicuous. 1) Avoid obscurity of expression; 2) Avoid ambiguity; 3) Be brief; 4) Be orderly (p. 24–27)

In communication, meanings are implicated by both the words uttered and the contexts in which they are uttered. In expressing intended meaning, speakers (and writers) depend on the conditions that govern conversation, relying on what Grice called the *Cooperative Principle*—the fact that others also observe the maxims of language. In instances where a maxim is violated, the listener (or reader) is compelled to look to the context to interpret intended meaning. Grice's maxims, together with the Cooperative Principle provide a way to understand how the meanings of *texts* are only understood in their *contexts*.

The maxims are not explicitly taught. Rather, as developing language users, children are in the process of gaining mastering these fundamental ground rules for language communication. The Unison Reading context provides a venue for students to apply their tacit understanding of what makes language effective to written texts. The more children have opportunities to read and critically analyze whole texts in the context of Unison Reading, the more skillful they become in applying this evaluative lens to their independent reading. Children read longer texts, such as chapter books, during independent reading time.

The Unison Reading method depends on the rule of whole texts to insure that children have an abundance of opportunities to interpret the meaning of texts in the context of social situations in which children can practice the pragmatic dimensions of literacy.

Unison Reading Grouping Practices: Breaking With Convention

Longstanding conventions dictate that children should be grouped on the basis of reading ability or reading level; and most conventional reading programs organize reading instruction according to reading level. One significant distinction between Unison Reading and conventional reading instruction practices is that Unison Reading prohibits the practice of ability grouping. In the Unison Reading program children self-select reading groups based on interest, in contrast to conventional reading programs where teachers are expected to assign children to instructional groups based on ability or reading level. This is done for several reasons. First, ability-grouping practices often reinforce patterns of social inequity found outside the classroom. Second, ability-grouping practices contribute to social stratification within the classroom, constraining the free interchange of ideas between children, and limiting their ability to learn from each other. Third, ability and leveled grouping practices reflect a narrow conception of reading based primarily on the ability to decode and comprehend texts decontextualized from the social situation. Unison Reading is fundamentally a pragmatic approach that emphasizes the social functions of literacy on par with the cognitive. Reading level is only one of factor of reading competence. Indeed, variation in ability levels within a group helps ensure collective learning within the group.

"Dynamic grouping" is a widely used grouping practice for reading instruction in which teachers "form small guided reading groups of students who have similar reading processes and can read about the same level of text" (Fountas & Pinnell, 1996, p. 98). "Dynamic grouping," like other forms of level-based grouping, is a practice that rests on the assumption that reading is foremost a cognitive process and that instruction should target competencies that prove challenging at the child's instructional reading level. The practice of grouping children by reading level, even if these levels are "dynamic," typically results in various patterns of de facto segregation in the classroom (racial, linguistic, cultural), and is antithetical to the tenets of democratic education and the inclusivity principle of Unison Reading. Segregation of any kind constrains the free interchange of ideas between children. Not surprisingly, the practice of ability grouping has been found to be detrimental to low-performing minority students and it has not been demonstrated to benefit high-performing minority students

(Lleras & Rangel, 2009). Ability or leveled instructional grouping results in the deprivation of learning opportunities.

Indeed, the "technology" of leveling children has fast become a lucrative industry. Virtually all instructional programs tout sophisticated methods of benchmarking, leveling, and monitoring the progress of children's reading levels. The lexile system is a widely used index of reading ability and text difficulty used to match readers and texts. According to Lennon and Burdick (2004), "A lexile is a numeric representation of a reader's ability or a text's difficulty. . . . When reader and text are appropriately matched, a reader can enjoy a comprehension rate of about 75%" (p. 3). Lexile measures reflect text difficulty based on syntactic and semantic challenges presented to a reader. But an excessive concern about lexiles or other indicators of reading level can become counterproductive when children equate proficient reading with high reading levels. The purpose and motivation for reading narrows to concerns like these: What level was that? What level am I at? What's your level? What level is she on? I'm a level M, what are you?

Liberation from leveled instruction

Conventional reading programs are designed around classical transmission models of pedagogy and a commodity conception of knowledge. When it is the teacher's role to dispense expertise or skill, there is a need to group children by skill level as a means to provide large numbers of students with instruction calibrated to an appropriate skill level. Unison Reading, springing from a different logic, allows for a different means of instructional grouping. Unison Reading frees us from the need to group children by level because it defines reading as the achievement of mutual understanding and necessarily involves dialogic thinking in the making of meaning. Decoding is just one means to an end.

Children have the capacity to develop as readers in much the same way they develop as speakers. Jerome Bruner (1982) explained that language development is "a subtle process by which adults artificially arrange the world so that the child can succeed culturally by doing what comes naturally, and with others similarly inclined" (p. 15). Just as we wouldn't restrict access to language learning formats based on the size of a child's oral language vocabulary or the mean level of semantic complexity of oral utterances, we don't limit children's access to group reading formats based on reading level.

Is text level ever emphasized within the Unison Reading approach? Yes. Children are encouraged to select reading materials that they can read independently during the independent reading portion of the reading block (an accuracy rate of 90% or higher is a common recommendation). Every child is expected to spend a large portion of their time during the reading block reading texts at an independent or slightly challenging level. But accuracy rates are not emphasized in the process of text selection for Unison Reading groups.

In Unison Reading classrooms, children who read at a relatively low reading ability levels participate in groups with more capable peers in reading challenging texts, with little notice to discrepant skills since the focus is on everyone contributing their effort to figure out what the author is saying. Even in groups that exhibit a great deal of variation in skill level in one domain (such as limited sight word knowledge or phonics knowledge), children show they are adept at participating to support one another's competencies. When skills come onto the table for consideration, advanced readers, in sharing their thoughts with others, have opportunities to sharpen their thinking by explaining their ideas, and delayed readers have opportunities to observe, imitate, and learn from others. More important, when anyone expresses intolerance for another's lack of understanding, the instructional agenda on the table justifiably turns to reinforcement of the "golden rule," since prosocial behaviors are valued on a par with phonological knowledge. Precisely *because* Unison Reading prohibits ability groups, it could be said that this method not only teaches children how to read, it helps them productively participate in civil discourse.

Interest groups and the inclusivity principle

The freedom to join groups based on text interests fosters an ethos of inclusivity that is vital to democratic education practices. Dewey maintained that democratic schooling practices should function to provide all members of society with access to "equable" educational opportunities that should not subordinate particular groups over others (Dewey, 1944). With a commitment to full integration in the classroom, and a definition of reading as a functional, dialogic, social process, Unison Reading groups include children from all levels of ability in routines that support learning for everyone.

The properties of inclusion and group diversity invite a much broader range of competencies than those typically associated with the curricula of conventional reading instruction methods that focus on mostly comprehension and skills (e.g., vocabulary, fluency, phonics and phonemic awareness). Since social, emotional, and relational factors are as important as cognitive competencies, all children come to every group on equal footing. Unison Reading groups create a space in which the low-functioning readers can exercise a range of competencies and succeed as well as their more proficient peers.

Reading is a form of social as well as cognitive competence, and social competencies are only learned in the company of other individuals who possess them. Diversity within groups in terms of temperament, empathy, language facility, literacy knowledge, socioeconomic status background, gender, race, and peer status become assets to learning because the Unison Reading protocol provides children with opportunities to think referentially and take from others who have different skills and perspectives. The greater the diversity of abilities and perspectives within the group, the more each group member stands to gain. Groups that include children from across the developmental span benefit everyone. Advanced children have opportunities to gain more critical awareness of their competencies through opportunities to explain their ideas, and delayed readers have opportunities to observe, imitate, and learn from others.

Since the protocol requires children to literally read the same words simultaneously, weaker readers are never left behind, but literally supported at every word. And because everyone is expected to contribute their questions and comments, and are praised for doing so, children are never stigmatized for not knowing something. The group process also supports high-achieving readers by giving them opportunities to practice explaining *how* they know *what* they know. Opportunities like these to use an increasingly sophisticated metalanguage for talking about what one thinks and the reasons for thinking it contribute to cognitive development in significant ways (Olson, 2007).

The rules of Unison Reading—that everyone literally reads the same word at the same time and offers mutual support when necessary—equip the group with the mechanism for cultural learning, allowing diversely leveled children opportunities to *succeed culturally in doing what comes naturally*, through cooperation and mutual support. The rules are designed to instill and support reciprocity and empathy in children.

Lauren Casion offers insight about how her fifth-grade students have been influenced by the power of learning in diverse groups:

> I think the most important thing is that these kids are becoming such sophisticated readers and learners in these social contexts. I really think Unison Reading has made even the lowest of readers think about reading in a new and enlightening way.

Inclusivity is good for everyone

Unison Reading is a protocol for group reading that allows children of all languages, abilities, and backgrounds to participate on equal footing in reading of a short text they find interesting. Because the pace is slow, even children with comparatively limited skills can participate with peers who have strengths in these areas.

Traditional ability groups or leveled reading groups that are organized to expose students to skills that are lacking tend to focus instruction too narrowly on subskills, and, in so doing, neglect the pragmatic and interpretive demands of reading. Unison Reading is based on the premise that "high-risk" or "low-ability" readers lack meaningful exposure to the English writing system and that ongoing supportive exposure to that system, primarily through socially mediated experiences, with students who possess target skills, will bring about desired literacy competencies.

Unison Reading integrates learning groups by involving children across linguistic, cultural, racial, and ability groups in text-based social practices. Children sort themselves into small groups of mutual interest and concern, reading texts of personal relevance, where they have the chance to triangulate their opinions and understandings to negotiate consensual meanings. Mastering the meanings of words and the ideas they reference, and other quirky English text features, becomes the object of engaged and critical discussion so that all participants contribute to the achievement of consensual meanings. And because Unison Reading involves all participants regardless of their status as good or poor readers, it serves as a democratizing practice in which all children are involved in learning experiences on equal terms.

Vocabulary and fluency: Important reading "pillars"

Fluency and vocabulary instruction have been identified as crucial pillars of successful reading achievement (National Reading Panel, 2000). Fluency and vocabulary instruction are addressed explicitly within the Unison Reading method.

Rethinking accuracy

Conventional wisdom suggests that comprehension begins to fail when reading accuracy falls below 90%. Practical pedagogical strategies, such as the "ten finger rule" (if a child misses more than 10 words on a page, the book is too hard) are based on this logic. The 90% formula is somewhat arbitrary, and the readers' intentions determine how much effort they are willing to devote to resolving confusion. Certainly accuracy rates of less than 90% are a cause of concern in independent reading for children who aren't yet aware enough to know when they don't know the meaning of a word or how to retrieve it. While this formula is applicable to independent reading situations, it isn't pertinent to Unison Reading, during which every point of confusion is scaffolded by the group in order to support achievement of collective understanding. The group can encounter more than one in ten unknown words and preserve the global meaning of a text since confusions are resolved as they occur.

Occasionally, a group will select a text that is simply so chock full of hard words or complex grammar that the extensive reasoning required to achieve meaning kills the momentum of reading. Sometimes when a text is too challenging because of complicated syntax or challenging vocabulary, frustration outweighs engagement, and little pleasure is derived from reading together. Though it is up to the group to decide whether to abandon a text, we encourage the children to come to this understanding themselves. I might say something like, "Reading should be satisfying. What do you think? Is this no fun? Why? Go ahead. Talk about it. You need to make your own decisions about which texts to pick. Just remember next time to preview to make sure it's something your group will like reading."

It takes time to understand: Rethinking reading rate and fluency

Reading fluency is a fundamental concern of reading development. According to the National Reading Panel (2000), "Fluent readers can read text with speed, accuracy, and proper expression" (Section 3, p. 1).

While speed, accuracy, and proper expression are all elements of fluency, many widely used reading assessments use only indices of speed and accuracy to determine fluency rate. For example, one measure commonly associated with reading fluency is the number of words a child can correctly read per minute. Target rates have been established ranging from about 50 words per minute in first grade to about three times that in middle school (Kuhn & Rasinski, 2007; Rasinski, 2004), and these are widely used components of reading assessment. Unfortunately, many children trained in reading programs that emphasize speed and accuracy tend to learn that they should read primarily to achieve speed. We have to take care that children aren't permitted to simply equate fast reading with good reading. When oral reading is too fast and mechanical, children miss important opportunities to learn how to use their voice in conjunction with text features—like syntax and punctuation—to interpret the text.

Reading speed and accuracy alone do not provide a full account of reading fluency. Reading prosody, an element of fluency, incorporates factors such as proper phrasing, cadence, emphasis, smoothness, pacing, and expression, helps give readers important comprehension clues (Kuhn & Rasinski, 2007). The National Assessment of Educational Progress (NAEP) uses a more complex rubric for fluency assessment that, in addition to speed and accuracy takes into account expression and phrasing. According to the NAEP scale, "Nonfluent" readers read word by word or in short phrases that fail to preserve language syntax. "Fluent" readers read in larger word groupings, read with expression, and, for the most part, preserve the author's syntax.

Unison Reading slows the pace of reading to give proper attention to grammar, punctuation, and word meanings. Children eventually learn that speed is not the point within Unison Reading groups. Some texts require slow, deliberative reading. Recipes and other forms of instructions, for example, demand a slow pace in order to understand ideas and sequential actions. Children need to be taught to use the gears of reading and to know when to shift down or up depending on the demands of the text. Some texts *need* to be read slowly and repeatedly to be understood. The demands of the situation determine the necessary rate of reading. Fluency instruction must be tied to consideration of the situation in which reading is being conducted.

In Unison Reading groups, the pace is slow enough to ensure that children can begin to interpret texts *while* they read and to let their interpretations inform the way that their voices sound. When a text is sufficiently challenging to the group, extensive conversation is required to develop collective understanding, and the reading rate might be as low as two to three words per minute. Because Unison Reading is conversation intensive, sessions might cover as few as 40–50 words in a 15-minute session, and sometimes fewer. While rate of correctly read words per minute is lower than would be the case in independent reading, conversation is fast paced and engaging.

Reading rate is not a relevant factor in Unison Reading sessions. But, fluency is. In Unison Reading, children are encouraged to tune their voices to the text by attending to punctuation and interpreting author's intent. In reading with children who sound as if their primary purpose is to reach the end of the passage, I breach the group and teach into the need to read with expression. I sometimes suggest rereading with dramatic effect: Pretend you're reading aloud to a young child. Or, I suggest, imitate Meryl Streep narrating the dinosaur film at the American Museum of Natural History (many of them have seen it). In a mechanical way, I say, "Meryl-Streep-does-not-explain-how-dinosaurs-became-extinct-sounding-like-a-robot. . . ." Then I try to the best of my ability to imitate the soothing, expressive voice of Meryl herself: "She reads the text with a lilting cadence and expression as if she were sitting by your side, whispering in your ear."

Fluency becomes the focus of attention when a child breaches the group because the sound of a text doesn't align with its intended meaning ("That doesn't sound right. You have to stop at the period."). Children also practice fluency when they reread whole sentences after they have resolved an unknown word within the sentence. Multiple opportunities to reread texts at the sentence level provide organic opportunities to practice reading fluency.

The challenge for most children—high- and low-functioning readers alike—is to know when they don't know something. When they first learn the protocol, until they learn to think on the spot, some children will be inclined to stop at every miscue, significantly slowing the pace of reading. If you feel they are stopping too frequently to repair every absent-minded miscue, you can suggest they think about the difference between miscues that deserve discussion and those that do not. Children should be encouraged to judge for themselves whether their miscues deserve attention (if there remains an unresolved confusion), or whether it was due more to an oversight that was picked up and mentally corrected on the spot.

Wrestling with words: An opportunity to grapple with the oddities of English

English is a nettlesome language to master, and Unison Reading is particularly well suited to provide support in learning to read English. The system of writing English—its orthography—bears traces of a kaleidoscopic array of cultural and historical influences. Orthorgraphy is very *opaque* (that is, unclear) compared to other languages with "shallower" orthographies that provide more explicit letter-to-sound correspondences (like French, Spanish, or German). Readers of English have to deal with a complex amalgam of spelling subsystems from Germanic, Norman-French, and Latin-Greek origin, which depart significantly from the one-letter-one-phoneme mapping principle characteristic of most of the world's alphabetic languages (Share, 2008). Due to the opacity of English, simple mapping rules do not apply, and readers must constantly rely on their lexical memory to read words that defy spelling rules (Dehaene, 2009). Children learning more transparent writing systems than English master the phonological abilities necessary for reading during their first year of instruction, while children learning English strive far longer (Share, 2008).

Phonics is a widely used and effective system of early reading instruction in alphabetic languages with a fairly clear and predictable system for decoding letters to sounds. But because English is so opaque—muddled with unreliable letter-to-sound patterns—phonics is a less reliable strategy for decoding unfamiliar words in English. In addition to phonics, children need opportunities to reason out why words in English look, sound, and mean as they do and exercise their memories for words. Because of its potential to support metalinguistic development through the supportive medium of oral language, Unison Reading is particularly helpful for children learning to confront the uniquely challenging demands of learning to read English (whether English is one's first or second language).

Once children have mastered the alphabetic principle, even well after they have a basic sight-word vocabulary of a stock of most high-frequency words, reading English continues to present immense challenges. One is the overwhelmingly large size of the English vocabulary. With over half-a-million words in the English vocabulary, and growing every day, English can never be mastered; it can only be reckoned with. We know that oral vocabulary and familiarity with the spoken form of words is an important factor in word learning, particularly for inexperienced readers and for irregular words (Ricketts, Nation, & Bishop, 2007). Because so many English spellings defy rules, you usually have to have heard a word in order to know how to say it. Oral vocabulary and familiarity of the spoken pronunciation of a large body of words is a necessary prerequisite for young readers to resolve the ambiguity they confront in attempting to decode unusual or exceptional spellings (Share, 2008).

Unison Reading offers opportunities for children to simultaneously hear how words are pronounced while seeing how they are used in the printed context. In Unison Reading sessions, because children are cautioned to "never miss a chance to make yourself smarter," they learn to take responsibility for learning how words are pronounced and what they mean. For example, the group of mostly ELL girls I sat with when they met for the third time that week had already collected 17 words on their Unison Reading Log. Involved in this fastidious level of word work, in the company of others whose collective reasoning takes the form of guesses, speculations, and past experiences, readers get to participate in precisely the kind of metalinguistic logic that will aid their independent reading.

Unison Reading formats give children ongoing opportunity to collaborate in deciphering odd features and pronunciations. These experiences help children learn to cope independently with the complexities of the English writing system, as illustrated by the following account of a reading group in which I participated.

Making meaning, one word at a time: An example

Brandon is the natural leader of a group of three friends in a sixth-grade classroom who've joined together to read an expository text about a castle in Ireland. Two of the boys scored in the bottom quartile on the state reading assessment and the other scored in the second quartile. Brandon is Hispanic, of Caribbean descent, and the most outspoken of the group. Wayne is African American. He was twice retained and is assigned to the self-contained special education classroom for content subjects. Kai is Chinese American, extremely reserved and task avoidant.

In reading the passage, Brandon and his friends were uncertain about 20% of the words they encountered and made quite a few miscues that required them to stop, discuss, and reread. These were good opportunities for learning, because each misstep became the object of critical reflection in conversation. Because the students themselves are expected to solve problems they encounter in their reading through the medium of conversation, the teacher's primary role in Unison Reading is to help guide and facilitate group processes and to help children gain a sense of responsibility in resolving problems in their reading independently.

> Brandon initiates this episode of Unison Reading, a protocol the boys have recently been taught and seem to have adopted for their own purpose. Brandon begins, "1-2-ready-go..." and the boys quietly read aloud. The boys read three words in unison before they all falter on the word *Cashel*, prompting efforts to sound it out and discuss its meaning, making reference to the featured photograph. Once they agree that *Cashel* is the name of the place featured in the photograph, the boys attempt to reread the sentence, stopping several more times as they hit glitches, fix errors, and reread, before finally reading the sentence fluently without error. The text is replete with words the boys don't know, including common but low-frequency words such as *ancient, nestled,* and *strategically,* and Celtic place names they could partially sound out but would not have previously encountered (such as *Sid Druim, Slieveardagh, Suir*). When we come to the word *strategically,* the boys look for familiar phonetic chunks within the word. I help them along, writing *stra-te-gic-ally* on a sheet of paper and guide them to sound it out with me. They do so handily, but blending the chunks into a word is a challenge for all. I say, "Let's stop and say it a few times." They do. Brandon gets it. But Kai and Wayne still have trouble.
>
> Three days later, when we meet again, Wayne still cannot accurately pronounce this word. "I can't say it!" he whines, smiling as he gently smacks his forehead.
>
> "That's ok!" I tell him. "This is exactly what you need to do when you come to a word you don't know how to pronounce. Admit to yourself that you don't know something, and commit to making yourself smarter. Now, say the word 'til you own it." The boys falter over seven words in a paragraph of 57 words, the last few accompanied by moans: "Oh, no, not another hard word!" But their complaints are more expressions of camaraderie and fortitude than helplessness. Before they conclude the meeting, their teacher, who has also joined the group, prompts them to consider a few questions: whether they want to continue with the text, what aspects of their learning they might want to share with the class during The Reading Share (another Genre Practice format), and which group process or reading process they want to improve upon during their next meeting. The boys offer the following responses: the session was "fun" (so said Kai, who, according to his teacher, rarely talks at all and never comments favorably on school experiences), they want to better synchronize their pacing next time, and they want to each read more loudly so that the others can hear and stay on the same pace.

A PEDAGOGY FOR READING

The cognitive revolution, an intellectual movement that began nearly sixty years ago, opened exploration into human mental functioning with a primary concern for the ways people make meaning from encounters with the world. We now understand that personal intentions are at the heart of learning and can only be cultivated in situations that promote agency, autonomy, and initiative. Though cognitive science discredited behaviorism as a sufficient explanation of learning, the classical transmission mode of instruction still prevails in classrooms where lessons are prescriptive, teachers tell students what to do, and "successful" students are those who do what they are told. In an effort to bring practice in line with contemporary cognitive science, Unison Reading offers a pedagogy for reading that emphasizes the cultivation of personal intentions on a par with the acquisition of skills and competencies.

4

"A Seat at the Table"

How Unison Reading Supports Every Child

Earlier chapters have explained how Unison Reading is highly engaging, abolishes ability grouping, prohibits a scripted curriculum, gives children agency, requires them to be primary decision makers in what they read and learn, and ensures that children learn what the standards require. Assuming you want to know how it works in practice, this chapter is an invitation to join several teachers who have implemented the Unison Reading approach in their classrooms at the Jacob Riis School. They will make space for you at their Unison Reading tables as they tell you about their work with children. Their stories offer answers to some of the common questions about Unison Reading, and will also expand your sense of the rich possibilities for reading instruction: not only to help kids read better, but also to provide them with opportunities to learn empathy and to achieve a general sense of well being about themselves. Welcome to the table!

■ RAISING STRONG READERS FROM THE START: UNISON READING IN KINDERGARTEN AND FIRST GRADE

Unison Reading is introduced to the children at the Jacob Riis School in Pre-K where the reading group exists more as an opportunity to learn to take turns, listen to one another, and share ideas than to teach children the written code. Of course, children attend to letters and their sounds as they collaborate around concept books, alphabet books, and simple rhymes. Unison Reading in Pre-K cultivates motivation and a *habitus* for reading. By the time children get to kindergarten, they are accustomed to the classroom social practices that support reading development.

Supporting a Delayed Reader

In the following account first-grade teacher Tara Clark explains how Unison Reading supports a child who is one of the lowest-performing readers in her classroom with an underdeveloped identity as a reader.

Thomas was held over in kindergarten and now is in the middle of first grade. I've had the pleasure of being his teacher his second year in kindergarten and now again in first grade. He has Speech and Language processing delays and is very passive. His learning is negatively affected by the challenges he faces. His struggles are especially evident when he reads independently. Even when reading familiar books, he makes a lot of mistakes and reading is not an enjoyable experience for him.

When he's in a Unison Reading group it's as if he's a totally different child. He takes so much initiative in so many different ways, especially if he's the leader. He has been gradually developing more leadership qualities that give him the confidence to speak up and share his thinking process with the group. Before Unison Reading, Thomas did not take initiative like he does now. There was no way for him to enter in and actively participate in ways that addressed his particular needs.

Unison Reading is so powerful for a reader like Thomas. It presents opportunities for him to feel empowered and make choices that affect his learning, to practice the very skills he needs to hone, extend his thinking and explain his thoughts, and experience reading as a fun and enjoyable. Now, Thomas actually chooses to spend his time reading with friends! He has made so much progress in terms of his overall approach and perspective and he is now open, willing, and excited about learning to read!

Benefiting All Children in Diverse Groups

Tara's second account exposes the deception of reading levels and how, in fact, all children possess multiple and varied abilities that intermingle with those of their group mates to support collective learning.

Children in a group of mixed levels and mixed language abilities were reading a book together about a cat named Tabby. When the group read together "Tabby was in the tree," some of the kids read *Tabby*, and some of the kids read *Taddy*. There was one particular student in the group who struggles with reversing the *b*'s and *d*'s, which is common among first graders. But she does it a lot, and she is working on fixing that. The kids all know this, so when she read *Taddy* instead of *Tabby*, another student stopped the group and explained to her that it's not *Taddy*, it's *Tabby* because there are two *b*'s and not two *d*'s and that she was again reversing the *b*'s and *d*'s.

Of the two students who were involved in this interaction, the student who read *Taddy* for *Tabby*, is a fluent English speaker and the higher reader in the group. She is a very successful decoder but she often reverses b's and d's. She also struggles with comprehension. The other student involved is an English language learner who struggles with the English language overall. Because of the opportunities Unison Reading allows, unexpectedly the English language learner followed in to *Taddy* and articulated her understanding of the higher reader's confusion of b's and d's. What a powerful learning opportunity for both readers!

Learning to Consider Others' Feelings

In another account, Tara explains how children themselves establish expectations for prosocial behaviors that then become conduits for new learning.

There was a very mixed group composed of a very high reader, a reader on grade level, and struggling readers. There were English language learners and fluent English speakers. We had an interesting dynamic going in this particular Unison Reading session. This group also had a mix of personalities. Some tended to be bossy and a little mean. When there was a breach in the reading, the children would use names, blaming others for making mistakes. Initially, the children did not seem to be bothered by this. As the teacher, I noticed some of the members starting to feel uncomfortable due to the blaming nature of the group process. I held my tongue. I wanted to give the children the opportunity to realize that this bothered them. I wanted them to authentically speak up on their own. The format and rules of Unison Reading encourage speaking up in circumstances like this so I was confident that if I just waited, someone in the group would speak up on the group's behalf. Finally, when another opportunity presented itself half way through the book, someone spoke up! "Wait. You shouldn't really be using people's names because that might hurt their feelings. You should say *someone said* so that we don't know who said it and we don't make anyone feel bad." It was so smart for this child to think that that was something important to bring to the group's attention. Her breach gave me a way to follow in and facilitate their understanding of how making someone feel bad stops the learning and the fun of the group, and how we're not willing to sacrifice learning. To this day they are really conscious about the way each person is participating and feeling in the group. They work together to maintain a promotive dynamic.

■ UNISON READING IN CONTENT AREAS: MAXIMIZING LEARNING IN MIDDLE SCHOOL

At the Jacob Riis School Unison Reading is used as a format for group instruction in all subject areas. The stability of the Unison Reading protocol provides a suitable container for children to explore a diverse range of text forms and genres across content areas since it supports critical thinking and the exploration of new concepts. Children routinely read math problems in unison, and Unison Reading groups serve as a context for science curriculum reading in many classrooms as well. The practice of Unison Reading embodies scientific thinking, as children confront uncertainty that arises from their reading with collective efforts to consider sources of evidence provided within the text. The Unison Reading group provides students opportunities to challenge, shift, or expand their perspectives.

In the next account, sixth-grade teacher Sabina McNamara tells of her sixth graders reading a text for social studies in which this kind of scientific thinking comes to life. Sabina teaches an integrated English language arts/social studies program.

Making Connections Across Cultures

We were studying Mesopotamia, which is current Iraq, and we were looking at a text about ziggurats, which are pyramid-type structures where the Sumarians used to go to school, pray, and pay homage to the gods. The kids are really, really jazzed up about this idea. A bunch of them for their projects are making models of ziggurats. Part of my job as a social studies teacher is to provide them with content. I can't do that every day of the week, so Unison Reading has to lend itself to content. But the kids get to choose what social studies topic they want to study.

Xiang, who is a high scorer on the Degrees of Reading Power, was a group leader for the week and picked an article on ziggurats from Wikipedia. Two girls, Lee and Serena, signed up for the group, and Shen was also in the group. Shen has a lot of focusing issues, and it's really hard for him to read or write independently. But he's really good in Unison Reading and just putting himself out there, admitting when he doesn't know something. He's really good at stopping the group and asking questions.

After they had already met for a session, Jeremy, who had just transferred from another class, joined in the group. Jeremy is a very reluctant learner. He has such an avoidance approach to school. Although he is low academically, he hates to admit when he doesn't know something. You can tell that he feels very insecure about himself as a learner. I thought it was really interesting that he joined this group.

This was a difficult text with a lot of difficult vocabulary. So in this group we've got Serena, who's in the middle level with Lee, and Xiang, who scores the highest, Jeremy who is the lowest scorer, and then Shen who has focusing issues. It's a really interesting group of five kids—totally mixed.

We start reading, and there are words like *Elimites,* and we're talking about time periods and dynastic periods. There's a lot of tough vocabulary, and Shen is openly stopping the group so that we can go over it. As we continue reading, Jeremy is sort of mumbling; Xiang, Lee, and Serena are reading just fine; and Shen is stopping the group.

This text had enough vocabulary to challenge everybody. Even a child like Xiang, whose parents had been very concerned that she wouldn't be challenged enough in Unison Reading because she's such a high flier, had a lot to learn from the text and from the group. There was something about the way the group was running that Xiang felt comfortable enough to stop the group because she didn't know a word. I could tell that Jeremy was watching that happen. When Xiang didn't know something, because she's like the know it all, then Serena said, "Oh I want to help you, since you always help me." Lee and Xiang are really good friends, so if Xiang stopped the group, Lee would join in. Then Shen, of course, joins in because he joins into any conversation anywhere that's going on about anything.

Before you knew it, they were all talking at once. Jeremy wanted to get involved—I could see that his body language was changing. He's speaking up a little more. He's giving his guesses and some of his attacks on the words. Some of his guesses are incorrect, but some of them are really smart. He would say something like, "I think it's this because earlier on in the text it said this." For him to have the opportunity to use that strategy and be right made him sit a little bit taller.

As they were reading, they found out that the ziggurats were compared to the Egyptian pyramids. Jeremy got up and walked away, and everybody's like, "Wait, where did Jeremy go?" He came back with this *National Geographic Kids* magazine, and it's got a picture of Chichen Itza in Mexico, which looks like a ziggurat. He comes over and says, "Look guys! Look! I found one! I found one!" He's a totally reluctant, avoidant learner, and he probably only saw that picture because he wasn't reading anything, he was just looking through that magazine and found those pictures. But he was able to then bring that information to the table, and then we used that magazine for the rest of the sessions as a guide. We worked off of that picture. He took the responsibility for keeping the magazine, bringing it to every session. He would say, "Ok, let's look at this again," because structurally they did look very similar—Chichen Itza in Mexico and a ziggurat. It was really interesting how Jeremy could find a place in the group as well as Xiang. They were feeling a little bit lighter, that they could admit when they didn't know something.

Developing Social Procedures

Shen had this problem of interrupting people. If somebody wanted to say something, he would jump in over people. I would point out, "Ok, Shen, there are other people in the group, you can't do that. You just steamrolled Lee. Look, Shen, you did it again." He'd respond, "Sorry." Then we'd do it again, "Serena was talking, Shen." These are all teaching points that I would teach into—relational stuff. Finally, I said, "Here's a way for you to be able to say, 'I want to be able to go next.'

(Continued)

(Continued)

Put your hand in the middle of the table and say, 'wait.' Then you can go." Shen took that, and he owned it: "Wait." Then everybody would put their hand in the middle of the table when they wanted to speak. They went in order that way, and they had discussions about "Well, no, my hand was first. Shen, you have to wait your turn."

The other group members were helping him to control his excitement, and I didn't have to do it anymore. It also helped a kid like Lee who lets people steamroll her. If someone interrupts her, she's not going to fight. This practice allows her to have a place to say, "I have my turn now."

For some reason, someone in the group brought up how to say "wait" in Chinese, "*don.*" So I said I know how to say it in Italian, "*aspetta,*" and in Spanish, "*espera.*" They all took that on, and for the rest of the session they were all saying "wait" in these three or four different languages. By our last session all of their hands were in the middle of the table to get started. As they counted, "one, two, three, *aspetta,*" they put their hands in and pulled their hands out.

Analyzing the Group Experience

They were like this family, this team unit that was created. It was just so meaningful because they learned a lot about ziggurats by digging into this text that was really difficult. If I were reading it on my own, I would have abandoned it. But when they knew it was their time to meet, everyone was really excited because of the social dynamic that was being built. Shen really felt like people were looking out for him but not in a demeaning way; they were really trying to be promotive. And Xiang felt that she didn't have to be this know it all; she had fun in the group. Jeremy, who was a reluctant and avoidant learner, felt like there was a place for him to be smart, and then he felt comfortable enough to say when he didn't know something. It was so cool to be a part of this session. You might think, "I have to teach this challenging text that the kids would hate," but they looked forward to it, and they loved it.

In the following week, when the groups had changed, Serena and Xiang were still together in the same group. They volunteered, "Oh, guys, we learned this thing, so if we all want to talk, we should put our hands on the table and take our turns." I didn't even have to teach that in a whole-group lesson. It was powerful enough that they spread the word about this way to take turns. They went on, "This is how you say 'wait' in Italian, this is how you say it in Spanish, and how you say it in Chinese, so maybe we should do it this way." There was so much that was now spreading to the other groups when they're moving on. We created this moment—they're going to move forward having that positive experience with them.

That's what Unison Reading is about. We can create spaces where kids can take risks and feel like they belong to something, and then they move forward a little bit taller and a little bit smarter. That really happened in this group.

ENGLISH LANGUAGE LEARNERS AND THE PULL OF A "COOL" TEXT

To learn English, one must be involved in ongoing social situations that support high levels of participation and language use. Unlike the traditional linear transmission curriculum where the English language learner is taught a program of skills in serial order, Unison Reading involves English learners as full participants in the reading group, alongside their native English-speaking peers. Because Unison Reading is premised on the belief that literacy competencies are acquired through active use, we expect that as ELLs assume full participation in reading groups, they will gain literacy competence. One factor that is essential to the acquisition of literacy competencies is the feeling of social connectedness that contributes to a sense of existential well-being that the upheaval of immigration can too easily threaten.

Jaela Kim, the fourth through eighth grade ESL teacher introduced in Chapter 2, has created an integrated, multi-grade model for Unison Reading involving student in all levels of English proficiency. Each week Jaela schedules nine slots. Children who receive ESL services take part in Unison Reading groups in the regular classroom and in the ESL "shelter" program. Leadership in the ESL Unison Reading program rotates, and children who are group leaders select a text of their choice. All students who are assigned to the ESL program can select any Unison Reading group based solely on their interest in the text, regardless of their grade level (see ESL Unison Reading Text Choices Figure 4.1). Thus, groups can have all levels of English proficiency, as well as all ranges of Grades 4–8. Children sign up for a group on Monday, and meet in groups Tuesday through Friday. Jaela explains how, after the implementation of Unison Reading in the ESL program, the children have gained responsibility to create their own schedules, cross-checking classroom schedules with time slots of their ESL Unison Reading group choices.

In the following account, Jaela narrates the story of Jun's group, including Joe, Ming, Lei, and Wen (see the descriptions of the group members in Figure 4.2).

Figure 4.1	ESL Unison Reading Sign-Up Board

Figure 4.2	Descriptive Characteristics of Students in One ESL Unison Reading Group

Jun—Group Leader	Joe	Ming	Lei (only girl in group)	Wen
Seventh grade 1.7 years in US Intermediate English First language: Mandarin	Eighth grade 8.2 years in US Intermediate English First language: Chinese	Fifth grade 1.7 years in US Intermediate English First language: Mandarin	Seventh grade 5.9 years in US Advanced English First language: Chinese	Eighth grade 3.5 years in US Advanced English First language: Mandarin
State English Language Arts Test: NA State Math Test: 3 (on a scale of 4)	Transferred into self-contained in seventh grade State English Language Arts Test: 2 (on a scale of 4) State Math Test: 3 (on a scale of 4)	100% attendance (never missed a day of school) Math State Test: 3 (on a scale of 4)	State English Language Arts Test: 3 State Math Test: 3	State English Language Arts Test: 2 (on a scale of 4) State Math Test: 2 (on a scale of 4)

Background

One day, Liang, an ESL student in fifth grade, came running into my room. "I have the coolest book, Ms. Kim. You're gonna love it! 'Cause it's not in your room, and it's in my room." I asked, "What is it, Liang?" He said, "Look it has all these cool genres. And there's one that's really cool called *Impossible Tricks.*" I told him, "I don't have time to look at it right now, but can you just leave it right there with a Post-it?" He said, "Ok. Well, make sure you look at it!" And he walked out.

Two hours later, Jun, a seventh grader, comes into my room, as always, during lunchtime. He was a beginner student in English last year and now is intermediate. It's almost like my room is a safe haven for him—I think it's like that for a lot of kids in ESL. When they need to relax, they all come to my room for a low-anxiety space. Jun comes in as usual with his iPod in his ears, listening to music. He strolls over to my desk, and he sees this magazine-like book. He says, "What's this?" I say, "I don't know, Liang dropped it off." So he opens the magazine, and he looks where the Post-its are and says, "This looks good. We should do this for reading." I respond, "If you want to do it, you can put it in the suggestion box for Unison Reading."

Then fast-forward a little bit: Jun is the group leader and puts this text, *Impossible Tricks,* up on the board. Liang walks in when it's time for him to choose a text, and he complains, "Hey, this is my text!" But he can't sign up because he's the group leader of another text. I told him, "Well, Liang, I guess you can't have the best of both worlds, but look at it this way: You've given Jun a really great text to do this week." He accepted this and told his friend, Ming, also in fifth grade, that there's this really cool text that he should sign up for. Ming gets really excited, and he comes into my room and signs up for the text. He says, "Liang told me this is going to be a really cool text." I responded, "Alright, cool, you know" (laughing).

Three other kids sign up—Joe, Lei, and Wen. Some background information follows:

- Joe is in the self-contained classroom, an eighth grader, new to our school. He came from another middle school in the neighborhood, where I think he was in another kind of program, but maybe not ESL.
- Lei is an amazing student. She's like my right-hand girl. She tells students, "You have to be responsible. You have to clean Ms. Kim's room 'cause it's not *her* room, it's *our* room, you know? We make the mess. We have to clean it up."
- Wen has been kind of reluctant for the past three years that I've had him, but I feel that he brings such a different perspective on everything. I look to him to give me feedback as a teacher, and he'll tell me the truth: "Ms. Kim, this share sounds cool, but when I do the share, other kids laugh at my work. The teacher doesn't stick up for me in the hallway when there is that student who is laughing or making fun of my accent." This kind of honest feedback from students helps me notice the way I need to change things and make other things happen. So Wen is really someone who is special to me as a teacher.

Learning Through Discussion

In the Unison Reading group we start off reading this "cool" text, and Joe is really stepping it up because of his participation in Unison Reading in his self-contained special education classroom. I was really looking forward to seeing him interact with the other kids.

I can't tell you what an amazing group this is. The things that they talk about, looking at the text, or looking at all the graphics. They're talking about where to start and what to do. In the text are all these different impossible tricks that you are told how to do. The kids are trying to do these tricks, and then I try. They claim to know this trick or that trick.

While they're having fun, they're asking such great questions, like about punctuation. "What is that? A dash?" Then they talk about the meanings of a dash. I remember that in another Unison Reading group we talked how usually whatever comes after the dash explains the preceding word. I just love using dashes in my writing, and I like teaching the kids about it because they think it's a cool punctuation.

Of course, Lei remembers what I said about a dash. She explains, "Well, a dash kind of tells you what the word in front means." I felt so bad because I told this girl that that's what the meaning of a dash was. Then the other kids agree, except for Joe, but no one's listening to him. So then they're going around like, I agree, I agree. But suddenly Wen isn't saying anything and neither is Ming. I said, "I'm a little confused. Is that really what it means?" Then all the students start to reflect again. That's when Wen offers, "Maybe it's just like a pause. Maybe it is just like a thought, like an idea." All of a sudden Wen seems to join the group, "I get it!" He's there to tell the whole group! Amazing! Meanwhile Ming, the fifth grader, feels a little intimidated because he's at a table with two eighth graders and two seventh graders. But he's sitting there nodding his head, and seems to be thinking, "Yeah, I feel kind of cool being with the eighth graders, reading this text. Liang was right—I'm glad I signed up for this text."

Outcomes

There are all of these little social things that are happening—the undercurrents of this group. They also monitor each other; for example, if someone says *under* instead of *underneath.*

Within the context of this Unison Reading session we were covering semantics and syntax. We explored the questions, what genre is this? What's the right word? How do we use how to's? How do we use procedurals? The standards came up. They didn't know what the standards were, so we looked at the standards and saw that they had to read a procedural text before the end of the year and know what it is and try to write one. From these 15 minutes of Unison Reading these students got such rich instruction in literacy that all builds off of their having fun with this text!

After the Unison Reading group I saw Jun go up to Joe and ask what grade he was in. And so not only is it giving them instruction, but it creates friendships. I've never seen such a powerful tool in the classroom, where students can start to make friends. It's so important for these ELL students to have these relationships, because often times ELLs are excluded and don't know how to socialize and make friendships. I almost feel like a lot of times they don't even want to leave that Unison Reading group because they get so into it.

See Figure 4.3 for Jaela's analysis of the Unison Reading group process.

RE-ENGAGING RELUCTANT AND AVOIDANT ADOLESCENT READERS

What happens when children *don't* receive an education from their very first years that supports their sense of competence and motivation, and lacks opportunities for them to feel like they belong in the classroom community? Can Unison Reading reengage children who have developed an oppositional stance toward school? Based on the equity principle (see Chapter 2), the true worth of Unison Reading as a theory and approach to reading instruction can only be measured by how well it meets the needs of the most vulnerable students. This account addresses that population.

Every teacher of habitually low-achieving students has found themselves challenged to find curriculum experiences that are engaging and simultaneously help students meet basic standards for reading achievement. Often, the depth of disengagement for these students prevents them from approaching most texts with genuine interest or curiosity.

Disengagement is a predictable adaptive response for a child who, as a consequence of chronic academic failure, feels relief, even contentment, in abandoning tasks that would otherwise certainly result in failure (Carver & Scheier, 2005). As "abnormal" as disengagement might seem, it is a psychologically healthy response in the person faced with unattainable goals, or who experiences, as Sapir (1932) put it, "alienation from an impossible world" (p. 242). If disengagement is the avoidance of threat, *approach* is engagement

Figure 4.3   Unison Reading Analysis With Inventory of Instructional Points

Unison Reading Analysis

Total breaches	8
Social Processes	50%
Genre	25%
Comprehension	12.5%
Decoding	12.5%

Members	% Participated	% Breached
Jun (Group leader)	87.5%	37.5%
Lei	50%	0%
Wen	62.5%	0%
Joe	62.5%	50%
Ming	50%	12.5%
Ms. Kim	75%	0%

Instructional Inventory

Social Processes	Genre	Comprehension	Decoding
Encouraging promotive behavior	Text form and purpose—Procedural	Visualize	Cross-checking
Fluency	Reader stance	Infer	Rereading
Pacing	Punctuation—Dash	Making connections	Monitoring for meaning
Affective factors	Genre layout—Use of visuals in text	Create images	Teaching others to self-correct
Interpersonal behaviors—Talking at the same time		Drawing conclusions	Self-correcting
Turn taking		Questioning	Phonics

in an activity with the perception of sufficient competence to be successful (Carver & Scheier, 2005). But reengaging disengaged students by creating achievable goals is not enough to help them succeed academically, which in addition requires sustained motivation and determination to meet normative academic expectations.

Unison Reading helps increase avoidant students' levels of approach because the activity itself is socially satisfying. Unison Reading also helps sustain motivation to strive to meet academic goals because the practice allows children to experience autonomy, competence, and relatedness to others in their reading pursuits (Deci & Moller, 2005; Deci & Ryan, 1985).

To put Unison Reading to the test, I'd like to invite you to one of the tables where Kerry Rutishauser and I collaborated in working with a group of middle school children in a self-contained special education classroom. The children in this group exemplify broader trends in the disproportionate representation of minority children in special education nationally. They are all boys. Three are Black/African American, one is Hispanic/Latino, and one is Asian.

In my role as school staff developer, I first met the boys briefly when I worked with their teacher the previous spring to help incorporate Genre Practice routines into his curriculum. However, I found the depth of dysfunctions in this classroom culture to be too profound to benefit from the weekly hour-long professional development residency that was used in general education classrooms. The collective personality of the group is aptly described by the indicators of oppositional defiance disorder (see Figure 4.4), since each of the children exhibited the majority of these behaviors (with the exception of revenge seeking, a behavior I never witnessed). The kids were disengaged from academic goals, and instead had well-secured goals to avoid academic work. Their basic needs for competence, autonomy, and relatedness (Deci & Ryan, 2002) were satisfied in socially inappropriate ways. They bonded through a *camaraderie of resistance*. Each of them, it seemed, made their own rules: "I won't be disruptive as long as I can do what I want, and you don't call home," for example. The kids walked the halls at will, left the room at will, engaged in side conversations when they pleased, napped, and fiddled. An extensive range of maladaptive behaviors had been established and secured over time within this classroom, and no single authority figure had been able to dislodge or readjust them.

One child in particular, Devon, concerned me the most. He never sat with me in instructional groups. While I tried to teach, he would either slap the table with his hand or a soft object (notebook, hat) or make the same repetitive yelp a number of times at equal intervals. I recall once calling his name five times before I said, "Devon, I've just had to call your name five times."

"I didn't hear you," he responded.

"I know you heard me. I know there is nothing wrong with your hearing. And of all the 700 kids I've worked with in this building, I've never had to call someone's name five times. I'm concerned that something else is the matter that you aren't sharing." He took the bait and lodged a few complaints about my working style. It was a start. But not enough since I was in the class so rarely. It was clear to both Kerry, the principal, and me that the depth of dysfunctions within the group could only be addressed by radically restructuring the self-contained classroom model.

Literacy competencies such as those delineated in the standards can only spring from a particular assortment of social situations that recur over time. Each of these boys, for a range of factors unique to each of them, were not successful in the general education classroom context. The traditional system of schooling, with its fetish for norms, is organized to sort out children who don't fit in. The system had created "abnormals" of these children, a term coined by the anthropologist Ruth Benedict (1934) who pointed out that

---

Figure 4.4   Criteria of Oppositional Defiant Disorder

- Frequent temper tantrums/loss of temper
- Excessive arguments with adults
- Active defiance and refusal to comply with adult requests and rules
- Deliberate attempts to annoy or upset people
- Blaming others for personal mistakes or misbehavior
- Often touchy or easily annoyed by others
- Frequent anger and resentment
- Spiteful attitude and vengeful

Source: American Psychiatric Association (2000).

"those who function inadequately in any society are not those with certain fixed 'abnormal' traits, but may well be those whose responses have received no support in the institutions of their culture" (p. 270). Nowhere does this truth stand out more starkly than in our system of special education, which, though not intended, has become the repository for all those children who unsuccessfully function within the narrow boundaries of normal academic behavior in highly teacher-controlled classrooms. The self-contained classroom in this school had become a kind of Siberia for the district at large (most of the children in the classroom had been sent from other smaller schools in the district where their "needs" could not be met).

To honor the democracy principle of Unison Reading, no single group can be subordinated to others. All must have equable opportunities to engage freely with other groups (Dewey, 1944). Self-contained special education programs that *segregate* one group of children from the free interaction with other groups violate basic tenets of democratic education by restricting activity to one classroom all day under the tutelage of one teacher (with the exception of special subjects like gym, art, and music), providing, essentially, a curriculum of deprivation. To satisfy the equity criteria, students in special education placements must be *integrated* to the greatest extent possible through creative programming.

At Jacob Riis, the self-contained program was restructured to integrate these children into the mainstream community. The self-contained special education classroom would now serve as a context for supplemental academic support. It was a base for the children who were mandated to be there by law. Since we were now defining literacy as a sociorelational process, and not a commodity, the goal for these children was not only to learn more *things,* but to establish and secure socially competent group behaviors that would enable them to successfully participate in Unison Reading groups, thereby providing widening circles of social interaction to help advance their reading abilities. The plan was for children to spend a portion of their school day in the self-contained setting, but to be mainstreamed into general education classes as much as possible. In essence, the goal of the Unison Reading program was to normalize prosocial, promotive behaviors in each of the boys so that they could successfully participate in a broader range of social groups.

Getting Started

In the fall of 2009 we began anew with a plan to reform the self-contained special education program. The group now included Isaac, Devon, Jaric, Joe, and Wayne, a student who joins the group on an occasional basis, as well as their teacher, who was new to the school. All of the boys speak non-standard varieties of English. With the exception of Joe, who scored in the 31st percentile on the DRP, all of the boys scored below the 20th percentile on the DRP. Devon scored in the 10th percentile. Two of the boys had each previously retained twice. Each of the boys had an Individual Education Plan (IEP) for various defined learning disabilities and behavioral problems that had previously interfered with learning including tapping, drumming, singing, roaming the halls, fiddling, aggressive behavior, and opposition to rules, boundaries, and authority.

In early September I had my first meeting with the boys and their teacher. Within minutes the session deteriorated into chaos, as I had suspected it would. I asked the boys to join me at a table for Unison Reading. All but one objected, but eventually they grudgingly joined. The few minutes were punctuated by petty arguments following my requests not to fiddle, rest heads on desks, interrupt, make noises, tap, or leave the table without permission. The teacher and I began issuing consequences, but within 15 minutes the boys were in a state of mutiny, and I resorted to calling the assistant principal on the phone to initiate our first "intervention," which I'll describe shortly. Unison Reading and other Genre Practice formats are premised on the idea that cognitive competencies emerge through social participation. In order to be able to take what one needs from the social situation, the child must be able to participate successfully. The group's behaviors needed to be realigned in order to benefit from instructional opportunities.

I developed the intervention protocol to help children whose behaviors have become too maladaptive to allow successful social participation. The intervention is a process that helps the child take responsibility to realign their behaviors with the normative expectations of the classroom. The intervention serves as a chance for adults to help engage the child in a process of behavior *realignment*. The format has roots in existential group counseling (see Yalom, 2005). As adults engage the child in a process of identifying "maladaptive" behaviors that cause unhappiness or suffering, they help the child gain awareness of these behaviors—what they feel like or how they are expressed. Invariably, the problematic behaviors are exhibited during the intervention session (such as making excuses, talking back, slinking under the table), thereby becoming accessible for reference in discussion. They help the child identify new goals for behavior and consequences for violations of commitments to new behaviors. Throughout the course of the intervention, children are involved in a dialog in which *they* identify behaviors and consequences, not the adults. In other words, the process allows children to take responsibility for their own actions and for the course of action that will unfold if they fail to keep their commitments. The intervention is now a regular format in the school conducted with children whose behaviors have become too problematic for the classroom teacher alone to handle. Throughout the course of the year, 15–20 interventions are conducted by the principal or one of the assistant principals.

Because academic literacy depends on social competencies and the ability to participate successfully in instructional groups, we could not let the situation in the self-contained classroom deteriorate unchecked. I left the room to find Kerry, the principal, to recommended an intervention meeting involving as many members of the school leadership and guidance teams as possible. Kerry convened a group including two assistant principals and two counselors to join us for the intervention. The boys were accustomed to getting away with ignoring their teachers, let alone me, *that lady* who comes in every week for an hour. It was important to send the clear message that the boys were accountable to the community at large, and the leadership was there to give them that message. The principals, counselors, and I convened in the hall, then entered the room. The boys looked surprised as we encircled them. A few of them collapsed their heads in their hands, complaining, "Oh man!"

Over the course of the next 90 minutes, I facilitated a conversation, involving the boys and the adults, in which I aimed to nurture the understanding that all of us, as members of learning groups, have commitments and responsibilities that must be met in fairness to the larger group. I reminded them that I'm responsible for being a leader of the group when I visit. In fairness to everyone, it is my responsibility to make sure that nobody compromises the learning of anyone else. I reminded the boys that they have responsibilities to themselves and each other. Every distraction one person causes detracts from others' opportunities to learn.

We spent a good deal of time letting them air their grievances. One of the boys was bothered that I had been inconsistent in my rules. I admitted that I had, but then explained why I changed the rule in response to the deterioration of group dynamics. All but one of the boys confessed they did not like being in a special placement. We assured them that we understood and that the program this year would be designed to help them be successful in regular classes; but we stressed that they had to uphold their responsibilities to be successful in the self-contained group in order to have the privilege of going into general classes. We discussed how, since general classes are so much larger, it is imperative that all children know how to follow the rules so that everyone's opportunity to learn is guaranteed. I laid on a little guilt: "Your parents work hard so that you can be at school each day. How do you think they would feel if they knew that someone was interfering with your learning? How would they feel if they knew you were interfering with others' learning? How do you think I would feel if I heard from a teacher that Liam [my son who attends the school] was interfering with another child's learning?" They agreed their parents would be bothered in either scenario.

We did a few rounds of consensus taking after every principle that naturally arose. "Do you understand how important it is for everyone to support the group and act in promotive ways?" There were a few protests and "yes buts." But overall the boys agreed.

Identifying problematic behaviors

I solicited their input on the behaviors that cause them to be distracted. At first they couldn't think of any. But when I told them I thought that was disingenuous and that the fact that we had to have the intervention in the first place is a stark reminder of the seriousness of the distracting behaviors. I told them they needed to be honest. It wasn't fair to the other 750 kids in the school to have all the counselors and principals taken from their usual work, and that they needed to take responsibility for their behavior in support of the whole. One said it's not okay to make people laugh. I pushed them: "So we agree it's not okay to tell jokes or make someone laugh. Is it okay to laugh when someone makes a joke?" "Yes," they argued. I responded, "But if you laugh at someone's joke, aren't you distracting the group?" And on and on. . . . Finally, we agreed on a list of behaviors that are disruptive. Once they got started in identifying and naming the behaviors, it didn't take long to come up with a comprehensive list that was charted and hung on the wall (see Figure 4.5).

Identifying consequences

"So what should happen if someone does one of these things?" "Nothing," they initially responded. "But wait, we have had to involve seven adults in a one-hour meeting because of these behaviors. Is it really okay for kids to do these things without consequences?" We had a long conversation about consequences. One of the boys assured me they wouldn't happen again. I said I hoped they would not, but I confessed that I suspected it would take some time to learn not to do the distracting things that had become routine. And I was fairly sure we would need to have clear consequences.

| Figure 4.5 | Problematic Behaviors |

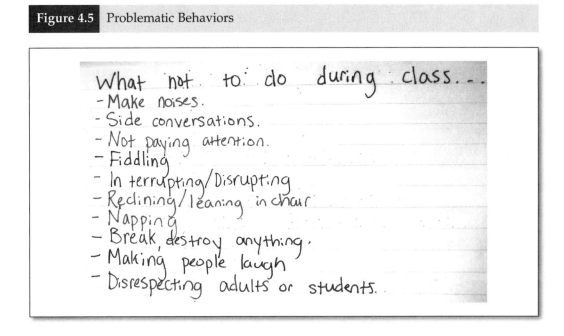

We negotiated, and our conversation went like this: "So is it okay to let someone disrupt the group?" I asked. "No, but the person should get another chance," a student suggested. "Ok, so how about a warning?" I suggested. "How about two warnings?" one student countered. "I think you're old enough to have only a single warning," I replied. Finally, we agreed on the progressively severe consequences listed in Figure 4.6

Committing to self-regulation and promotive behaviors

I then began to breach another point: "Okay, so the problem we've been having is that sometimes some of you start doing something that's distracting, and you get into a cycle where you can't stop. And before you know it, you've earned five consequences, and it's time to call home. It seems that there's something that's getting in the way of your telling yourself to fix your behavior. Do you know what I mean?" Predictably, some of the kids expressed certainty in maintaining self-control. "Ok, but what if you slip up? We have to have a plan in case that happens. What strategies do we need to figure out to help you regulate yourself?"

"Can I make an observation?" I added. "The problem is that you always leave the responsibility to your teachers to address the problematic behavior. Then what happens is the problem becomes a conflict between the teacher and the student. And when this happens, nobody seems willing to talk about it. Then there's an argument that takes time away from everyone's learning. What are you going to do about that?" They countered that they couldn't be blamed for other kids' behavior. I countered: "No, but if you are responsible for the welfare of the group, do you have a responsibility to tell someone when they are doing something that is distracting to you and the group?" This was a novel thought for some of them. We talked more to allow the idea of responsibility to the group to settle.

After more conversation and urging them to consider their responsibilities to themselves and others, the kids agreed to do the following: (1) When things go in the wrong direction, we will be willing to talk about it, and (2) If some members are disrupting my group, I will ask them to stop, and tell them they are bothering me.

I suggested the teacher make a written contract (on the spot), and we passed it to each boy to sign. This contract, containing the commitments listed in Figure 4.7 and witnessed by seven adults, was posted in the classroom.

Figure 4.6   Progressively Severe Consequences

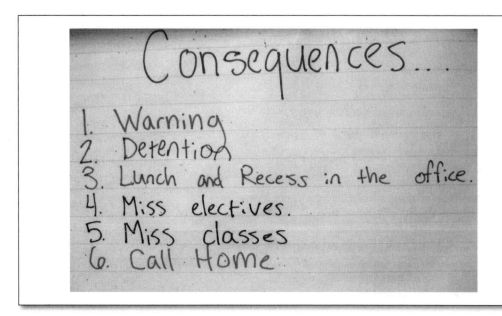

Figure 4.7	Commitments to Class Rules

We agree as a class . . .

- I will do Unison Reading for 15 minutes every day without argument.
- When things go in the wrong direction, I will be willing to talk about it.
- If some members are disrupting my group, I will ask them to stop, and tell them they are bothering me.

When the intervention was concluded, we had established a commitment on the part of all the children to make an effort to successfully participate in the group process. This intervention protocol has become standard practice for children across the school who demonstrate oppositional/defiant or other inappropriate behaviors. Once children can participate in groups successfully, they can benefit from opportunities to learn from the group.

Two Steps Forward, One Step Back

I met with the boys for a Unison Reading session a week after our intervention meeting. A couple greeted me with disappointing sighs. The boys had selected a text about a professional skateboarder. I breached the group 97% of the time. The instructional points were mostly related to relational processes followed by comprehension issues having to do with my own lack of understanding of the text (as it was a feature article about a professional skateboarder, *I* was the *low* reader of the group). The boys were generally impatient, inclined to rush through reading, hesitant to discuss points raised, sarcastic and disrespectful toward me and each other, and forgetful of the rules. At one point, just as I breached the group with a question, Isaac rolled his eyes and gasped in irritation. I explained my need to understand. Several minutes later, Wayne, an occasional visitor to the group, breached the group with an inaudible question. I asked him to repeat it, but he refused. I let it go, but went on to make a point about the need for patience and empathy in the group. I said, "Luckily, because I'm older and I've worked with a lot of kids, I could gather up the courage to breach the group and go up against Isaac's look. It made me feel embarrassed and a little insecure when you rolled your eyes at me and gasped. But luckily I asked my questions anyway, and we got the chance to learn the difference between *perfikt* and *perfekt*. But I worry that when each of you has a question you might be too intimidated to speak up because you're afraid someone will roll their eyes or make fun of you, and that doesn't feel very good." Each problematic behavior had to be fully addressed as it occurred, and we read only several paragraphs. The session lasted more than 30 minutes.

In order to sustain the positive behaviors that we had worked hard to establish in the group, Kerry began meeting with the boys and their teacher several times a week for Unison Reading. As was the case with the Unison Reading group I described above, Kerry's initial sessions with the boys focused primarily on social behaviors and helping the children to adhere to Unison Reading rules. Kerry elaborates:

Jaric had his hood over his head for a long time. So I said to the group, "What do we do when one member of the group isn't reading, isn't following one of the rules? What can you say to that person?" I was trying to teach them responsibility for each other—that this is a social process and they're in this together. I really emphasized how reading socially is really powerful and how they're going to learn a lot. Then they started calling out, "Jaric, are you gonna read with us?"

Initially Joe never breached the group and rarely participated, probably because his comments were typically followed by sarcastic remarks and impatience on the part of the other boys. But over time, as prosocial behaviors were established in the group, Joe began to speak up, even becoming a group leader. The other boys began to rely on him to identify confusing words or ideas.

Fluency

We finally got everyone to sit at the table and read in unison, and then the big hurdle was that Isaac would read robotically and quickly. Then they would have to stop and address that. We'd start again, and then Devon would read too fast. Joe, the ESL student, would have to say, stop, you're reading too fast, you need to slow down. Then we had to talk about why is it important to read slower in Unison Reading and to read periods and commas. The fluency issue came up right away. And I think that's pretty common across the classrooms.

Securing Promotive Behaviors

Joe would follow the rule of stop when you have a question or comment, and he would stop the group a lot. In the beginning, Devon would stop the group a lot too. But a word like *ominous* may take 5–10 minutes to figure out. We chunk it out and sort of figure out how to pronounce it. Then how are you going to figure out the meaning? I would teach into looking in a dictionary. They would have guesses about what it means. Now they have to put it back in context so it makes sense.

These boys have spent years in their classrooms being passive and disengaged. But with Unison Reading you have to be *on*. It's intense. It's something they were not used to. So a lot of times when they were getting used to Unison Reading, they would get exhausted. They'd said, "I don't like stopping; this is tiring." Devon wanted to just push through. When Joe tried to continue trying to stop the group, they'd get mad at him. There were a couple of sessions where we had to talk about why Joe might be stopping. "He's ESL; he might be stopping on a word you know, but he doesn't." We had to really talk about how to be promotive in a group. "Dissing each other for stopping is not promotive."

One of the conversations we still have is Devon doesn't want to stop at everything he doesn't know. I've had to teach in to the rule is that you have to stop when you don't know. I show them how powerful that is. We have all the words they didn't know listed on the board. I said, "Look at all these words you know. You know *prosecution*, you know what *lawyer* means. These are words that give you power in your life. These are words you have to know. Had we not stopped at these words to talk about them, you wouldn't know these things." *Ominous* came up in another text that they chose. They were pretty excited that they recognized the word in another context later on, and they knew how to pronounce it.

What I noticed was that the things that I'm working on with the students in the self-contained classroom are no different than what I have to work on when I go into the general education classroom. Even with the honors kids (who aren't in honors anymore because I dismantled that program last year), I have to teach the same lessons—fluency, reading too fast. They want to read fast because they think they're really smart and they can read fast. They don't stop at words they don't know probably because they don't want to admit they don't know. They don't think that they need this.

Steady Progress

The boys made tremendous progress with their work with Kerry, as was evident in a comparison of two 10-minute sample Unison Reading records from September and November (see Figure 4.8). Notice in September that I breached the group 93% of the time (Wayne breached once). Not only was it I who breached the group in September, but all of the comprehension instructional points had to do with my own confusions. The boys were all passive, except for Devon, whose participation consisted mostly of challenges to my comments and questions.

By November, the boys assumed far greater responsibility for facilitating the group. There is greater distributed participation, and each participant readily breaches the group. The boys were now raising questions about the text and allowing their questions about the technical features of language to surface in discussion, evidenced by the increase in their breaches from 7% in September to 100% in November. Kerry participated 75% of the time, but most of her turns were in the form of her own questions or responses to Isaac's prompts. They had stopped being defensive and hiding their confusion and had begun to demonstrate humility and trust in the group to raise questions when they were confused. The instructional points were now balanced across the domains of Social Processes, Comprehension and Decoding, and all instructional points were raised and addressed by the boys themselves. Their improved ability to function as a group, consistent practice with reading, and opportunities to learn new things in the context of Unison Reading significantly impacted the boys' performance on the Degrees of Reading Power assessment. After a year of the Unison Reading program, the boys gained an average of 12.2 DRP units (over six times the national average rate of growth for eighth grade). Devon, who initially refused to sit at the table, gained 23 points on the DRP between September and June.

It is critical to emphasize that these changes are a result of consistent instruction. Kerry and the other boys' literacy teachers (their special education teacher and the general education teachers) coordinate their efforts to hold the boys accountable to the agreed-upon obligation to participate every day and to give them consequences when they fail to do so. For example, one rainy afternoon in February, a full six months after the daily Unison Reading routine had been established, two boys showed up in Kerry's office to report for detention. Carlos Romero, the assistant principal asked, so why are you guys

Figure 4.8 Comparison of Unison Reading Records From September and November

Unison Reading Analysis—September

Total breaches	14
Social Processes	50%
Genre	0%
Comprehension	35%
Decoding	15%

Members	% Participated	% Breached
Cynthia	100%	93%
Devon	78%	0%
Jaric	14%	0%
Isaac	71%	0%
Joe (ESL)	0%	0%
Wayne (visitor)	21%	7%

Instructional Inventory

Social Processes	Genre	Comprehension	Decoding
Process for delegating leadership Following rules/participating Distracting behaviors Unison Reading rules Reading in sync Losing place/staying in sync Pacing		Retelling Background knowledge Vocabulary/new concept Vocabulary pronunciation Questioning Thinking while reading	Reading plurals in Standard English

■ ■ ■ ■ ■ ■ ■ ■ ■ ■ ■ ■ ■ ■ ■ ■ ■ ■ ■ ■

Unison Reading Analysis—November

Total breaches	8
Social Processes	3 50%
Genre	0%
Comprehension	4 35%
Decoding	1 15%

Members	% Participated	% Breached
Kerry	75%	0%
Devon	63%	13%
Jaric	50%	0%
Isaac	100%	38%
Joe (ESL)	63%	50%
Wayne (visitor)	21%	0%

Instructional Inventory

Social Processes	Genre	Comprehension	Decoding
Process for delegating leadership Following rules/participating Promotive behaviors Unison Reading rules (group leader needs to decide when to go on) Checking in with others "Joe, do you get it?" Losing place/staying in sync Pacing		Meaning of *The Deuce* Background knowledge Number of touchdowns—good or bad relative to position played and height (questioning, synthesizing, drawing conclusions) Vocabulary/new concept: *seasons* as term used in sports Vocabulary pronunciation Questioning Thinking while reading Meaning of acronym USSSA	Decoding *deuce* Reading plurals in Standard English

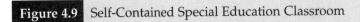

Figure 4.9   Self-Contained Special Education Classroom

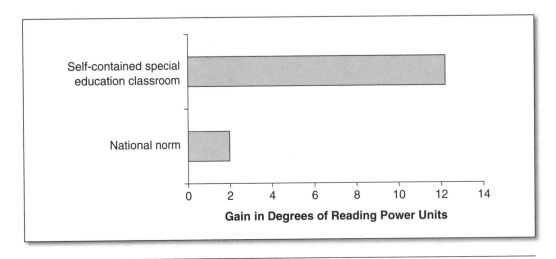

Note: Number of students = 5. Scores are reported on a 100-point scale.

here today? One sighed and admitted, "We weren't participating . . . we weren't breaching." Two steps forward, one step back.

RE-ENTRY: MAINSTREAMING STUDENTS WITH SPECIAL NEEDS INTO THE GENERAL EDUCATION CLASSROOM

In the previous section we have shown what Unison Reading does for students in a self-contained classroom who have had a history of serious learning challenges. But another challenge faced by countless schools everywhere is how to meet the needs of the most vulnerable students within the context of the general education classroom. To what extent can Unison Reading be used in the general education setting to guarantee that all children flourish? As the previous chapters have explained, Unison Reading is an instructional method that allows all children, who might read independently at different levels, to nonetheless participate in collaborative dialog around texts and enjoy equal learning opportunities.

In the following account, Kerry Rutishauser will lead us into the general education classroom where Devon, whom you met above, joins a Unison Reading group with students who were formerly in the now-dismantled honors program.[1] Kerry is helping Devon transition back into a mainstream general education classroom. Devon happened to be the group leader for this session, and had selected a text that he had previously read with his classmates in the self-contained classroom on "Snapple Facts," a list of retired trivia questions and answers from the inside of Snapple lids. Kerry explains,

[1]The middle school previously had an honors program and a general education program. These programs essentially segregated the middle school by race and class. Students in the honors program were overwhelmingly White and Asian and students in the general education program were overwhelmingly Black/African American and Hispanic/Latino. The Genre Practice methods, Unison Reading in particular, provide a means by which children of differing abilities can be integrated for instruction. During the 2009–2010 school year Kerry Rutishauser dismantled the honors program and integrated students from both programs in all subjects but math, where an honors track was retained.

I joined on the second day that Devon's group was doing "Snapple Facts." The group is comprised of two former honors students, Derrick and Tonya; Ellen, a student who had been in a general education classroom the previous year; and Devon, who is a student in the self-contained special education program. Right away we had social processing issues. Although Devon is the group leader, Derrick, one of the former honors students, starts the group. Tonya, the other former honors student says, "Wait, this is Devon's article." I interrupted the group to teach into this, thinking it was disrespectful to Devon. We had to have this conversation about how Unison Reading is a social process and that they really learn how to comprehend at a higher level when they have to come to a mutual understanding of what words mean. And in order to do that they have to have these social processes in place. I asked Derrick, "How could you have started the group differently if you knew this was Devon's article?" He stayed quiet and he wouldn't even look at me. He was annoyed at me interrupting. When he didn't respond, I said, you could say, "Hey, Devon, since this is your article and you were group leader yesterday, do you want to be the group leader again today? That would have been promotive rather than just starting the group without checking with him. Can you say that to him?" And Derrick responded under his breath, "It sounds so robotic." I said, "What did you say?" He said, "It sounds so robotic because you're giving me the language." And I said, "Well, you didn't have the language! It wouldn't feel that way if you had the words. You had to know."

I'm teaching the advanced readers the exact same prosocial behaviors as I did in the self-contained classroom. Devon is watching me do this, and I think that made him feel more equal. He sees that the same kind of teaching goes on in the mainstream. And actually he's more competent than some of the other kids.

The other issue that happened in this group was that the kids weren't breaching—same as with Devon in the self-contained classroom. I had to really teach into that. "Wait, you didn't stop at that word. Do you know what that word means? No. Then why didn't anybody stop?" Devon would see that I have to do the same kind of teaching with the honors kids as I do with him in the self-contained special education classroom. He's actually pretty competent at it now.

We can't ignore the interpersonal dynamics going on in groups like this, and we can't ignore that the kids know these dynamics are going on. First, these kids know they've been segregated in school, and they have the issues that come along with that. The ones that have been in the lower groups feel inferior and the ones that have been in the higher groups feel superior and wonder why they are now in mixed groups. In a lot of ways they may be better readers. But in this case, it was one of the higher readers who didn't have the language to communicate in the group. In this group, there were also racial dynamics. That's my assumption. But Tonya, who is Black, was quick to point out that Devon, who is also Black, had been ignored by Derrick, who is White. Unison Reading is socially inclusive, and as a teacher you can't ignore the dynamics that come to the table.

Derrick's resistance is typical of what you see in some students in Unison Reading groups in middle school. If you as a teacher don't address the resistance, Unison Reading will fail. Derrick was resistant. He was angry at having to read in the group; he wanted to read by himself. And I had to address his resistance.

Reading is a form of social activity, and reading skills come about through competent participation in literacy activities. From this standpoint, the "shelter" programs—such as the self-contained special education classroom or the ESL classroom—exist to help children gain competence and confidence in the social practices that will help them participate successfully on an equal footing in the mainstream classroom.

■ UNISON READING IS GOOD FOR EVERYBODY: THE ADVANTAGES OF DIVERSE LEARNING GROUPS

The previous accounts show how Unison Reading provides a strong scaffold for children with limited or delayed reading literacy. But Unison Reading has also proven to be a powerful means to ramp up literacy awareness in high-achieving children by giving them opportunities to think metacognitively and to bring into full consciousness existing tacit understandings about texts. Unison Reading is good for all children involved because each brings a unique set of strengths and perspectives to the reading experience. Kerry continues with an account of her work with another Unison Reading group.

> There was another group I had with two former honors kids and an ESL student, Kim. She was also getting Unison Reading in the shelter program in ESL. For ESL kids to speak up is a big issue, and Kim wasn't reading loudly enough for the other members of the group to hear, but they just kept going. I called them out on that. And then I taught them, "What do you say to Kim if you don't hear her? 'Kim, could you please speak up because we can't hear you.' Why didn't you do that? That's a rule." I reviewed the rules. "Ok, let's go back and try it again."
>
> The text the group was reading was an article from *AM New York*, a newspaper given out on the subway. The article was about remarks from the New York State attorney general, and it was really hard reading with some difficult syntax. In the beginning of the article, they read right through *attorney general*, although they didn't know what the words meant. They read through some other words like *scam*. I stopped them: "Do you really know what *attorney general* is?" None of them did, but none of them would admit it. So I said, "Why didn't you stop the group? You read through it. You even reread it. You still don't know what *attorney general* means." We had to go through that.
>
> At one point Kim sort of put her hands out to try to stop the group. She didn't know what to do with her hands. I said, "Kim wants to stop the group. Kim, you've got to say, 'Stop'" (smacking my hand on the table). She whispers, "Stop." I said, "No, *stop!*" (smacking the table). "Say it! Do it!" She tries again, "STOP!" (lightly smacking the table). "Great, do it again! (laughing). That's what you all need to do!" They're afraid to stop the group. You have to teach into that!
>
> I was pretty aggressive with that group. At the end of the session, I said, "We've been together 20 minutes, and we've learned what *attorney general* means. Had you stopped at the other words, you could have really addressed them. But you went right over them. So now you still don't know what this passage means."
>
> At first, some kids *really* resist stopping at the point of confusion. If you don't teach into it, follow in, and make sure they do it, this approach won't work. The higher level of comprehension comes when you have a mutual understanding about what individual words mean. Often times I have to teach into, "So you just gave an interpretation of what you thought *ominous* meant. But everyone just looked at you silently. You have a responsibility to make sure you have a mutual understanding with the group. What can you say? So they start to learn how to talk to each other.

■ "UNISON READING *MAKES* TEACHERS *READING* TEACHERS": WHAT WE OURSELVES CAN LEARN AT THE TABLE

Throughout this chapter we have heard accounts by teachers of the potential of Unison Reading to impact their students. I'll conclude this chapter with an explanation about how Unison Reading has the potential to favorably impact teaching.

Kerry Rutishauser commented, "Some programs don't require any expertise from the teacher. They're scripted. The program tells them what to do. It is quite amazing how Unison Reading *makes* teachers *reading* teachers." How does Unison Reading make teachers reading teachers? Sixth-grade teacher Amy Piller explains how the boots-on-the-ground nature of assessing reading in the moment helps her understand the challenges her students face, particularly children who experience difficulty reading.

> By participating in Unison Reading with struggling readers, I watch them problem solve in a manner specific to the given sentence they are deciphering. Watching them do this helps me to identify what structures trip up their understanding in a boots-on-the-ground kind of way. Watching them make meaning also helps me understand how their minds work. Somehow after meeting with them in Unison Reading I feel like I have a better grasp about what types of explanations will make sense to them. Unison Reading also helps me to understand their struggles. Just recently we were reading an article about Yu-Gi-Oh, and I had to breach repeatedly to try and understand the characters' motivations, which were obvious to the kids in the group who play the card game and read the graphic novels associated with it. At some point amidst fruitful conversation Roberto turned to me and said, "Now you know what it's like when I try to read." We both laughed, and I think he felt like maybe, just maybe, his challenging relationship to reading wasn't such a bad thing after all.

The practice of Unison Reading depends on astute observation and careful record-keeping. It is, essentially, a pedagogy of observation and response. We watch for the "X Factor" to come to life, follow in, and make sure that someone always closes the breach (or that we do). The method requires teachers to become involved in a process of careful observation to detect how children are participating together in the group in order to make sense of a text. And because observations are closely aligned to well-established domains of reading, over time, teachers gain expertise about reading development simply through the daily practice of making systematic observations of children's reading in relation to standards, documenting these behaviors, and acting on them. Lauren Casion comments on how practicing Unison Reading has helped her readjust her stance as a teacher of reading.

> I've gotten better at stepping back and letting it unfold for me. And I jump in where it's necessary instead of me being the person who stops the group or setting the course for where the conversation is going to go. I think that the students very much inform the direction of the conversation. In terms of instruction, I think that a lot of the time they are doing these things . . . making their own instructional points. But it's my job to follow up. Name it for them. What they just did and all the different steps they took to get there. So it's not so much me saying oh, we can make an inference about what the character is feeling. They are doing that, but maybe they aren't aware that they are, in fact, making inferences. So I come in and say, well look at all these things that you just did. That's you as a reader making inferences about a character.

The Unison Records themselves become a critical source of competence feedback for teachers. As you document students' competencies and achievements, you will have access to a growing body of evidence of your own competence and effectiveness as a reading teacher. Through the process of documentation and reflection, you'll develop expertise and confidence in reading pedagogy. The more you practice Unison Reading, the better you'll get at teaching reading, and the more you'll appreciate the principles and routines of the Unison Reading model. This cycle of learning will benefit both your students and you.

Superheroes

By Amy Piller

Many kids go unshielded
from many taboos,
becoming unclear
in purpose
on learning,
how to read,
why to care,
what to do.

On reaching the appropriate age
to know enough
to be afraid
of what is revealed
when they speak up,
they go
silent
(minus making a scene,
getting a laugh, being at ease
with being left out
of what seriousness means).

Suddenly they want to read (what a coup)
an article about "Halo Two,"
a long, laborious, video game review,
hold your groan, you seek escape daily,
in success's pursuit.

Wondrous wonders when someone says,
"What does that mean,"

"What, sequel?" another deigns, "Oh *you* know like . . ."
then trails away,
alone unable to explain.

So someone steps up, "Like one more,"
the smart contagion swells,
the snowball gains core—
"A series," another sputters
and finally the unsure one

sure enough,
"It's number two,
like the title,"
(with that chest puffed-up
"duh" look in his eye)—
at long last, with confidence,
he speaks up.

Right, they agree, and read on
stumbling over "innovation,"
which they say is like sequel
only unrelated to what came before.

Finding this funny they laugh
the uncomfortable laughter
of teenage achievement—
a joke to be made
for every promotive
moment gained.

Then they discuss whether they want to be
heroes in this future
world or not.

"Not if I was eleven."

"Well how old would you need to be?"

"Twenty."

Now I find myself amused.

They turn around quickly
look at me confused
equally invested now
in weighty contemplation—
nothing funny about their potential
saving the world
nine years from now.

Education's promise persists;
the posturing
of prospective superheroes.

5

Conclusion

Unison Reading as
Consciousness Raising

It is a uniquely human capacity to work collaboratively in relatively extensive social groups to accomplish common goals. Indeed, some believe that the human brain evolved to be two to three times larger than other primates so as to manage the comparatively complex social interactions required for our survival (Dunbar, 1998). Our special brain power enables us to understand the mental states of others, and thereby manage differences, exploit collective strengths, solve problems creatively, and achieve our imaginative possibilities. Our capacity to use language essentially to think how others think allows remarkable individual and group achievements. We're wired to overcome obstacles by reaching out to others in order to solve problems and pursue our goals.

Though accepted in the behavioral and biological sciences, this social paradigm hasn't influenced conventional pedagogical practices. Classical linear transmission pedagogies still dominate schooling practices and discourage and inhibit collaboration as a primary means for new learning. Within the realm of reading instruction methods, the student is treated as an isolated entity and is taught reading as a technical skill. Children are typically grouped according to what they know or don't know in relation to target skills, depriving them of their innate capacity to learn from others in order to compensate for their lack of knowledge. This curriculum of deprivation dominates the field of reading education, where an elaborate and technical array of "scientifically based" practices have been developed to raise individual reading achievement. But many of these practices are boring and uninspiring to many children. In reality, schools often deprive children of what they need to become better readers because we prevent them from taking part in social interactions that expand their capacities as readers. If recognized at all, social interaction or collaborative efforts are marginal variables in the equation of achievement.

Traditional Western schools have functioned according to a logic that goes something like this: activity X requires Y skill. If Student A lacks Y skill, administer Y-enhancing treatment for a specified time interval. Reevaluate Student A's performance on X activity after prescribed treatment. If Student A's performance is not improved, repeat treatment or administer alternative treatment. This logic has been operationalized into conventional reading practices that have proven to be problematic on several levels. They often

- segregate classrooms by grouping children by ability levels, limiting the democratic potential of education;
- rely on "inside the head" theories of psychology (such as cognitive and componential theories of reading), neglecting cultural transmission and intermental learning processes that are often more instrumental in learning and development;
- fail to exploit contemporary theories of learning, competence, and motivation; and
- bore and alienate some children and in turn undermine academic development.

Classical transmission modes of pedagogy, with their misguided view of learning as a direct outcome of teaching, hold a relatively uncontested dominance in schooling practices. And recent reform initiatives have placed a heavy emphasis on skills instruction with inconsistent results. The U.S. federal government's billion-dollar-a-year Reading First initiative, designed to ensure that all children are able to read by third grade, failed to impact reading comprehension in Grades 1, 2, or 3 (Gamse, Jacob, Horst, Boulay & Unlu, 2008). Similar reform policies carried out in the U.K. that emphasized basic literacy skills showed similar limitations in raising literacy achievement. An intensive British report sponsored by the University of Cambridge found that the last decade of reforms that emphasized a focus on literacy skills not only failed to achieve mandated goals, but also bored children and demoralized teachers (Alexander, et al., 2009). Skills-oriented curriculum policies have done little to improve adolescent literacy rates in the U.S. where progress in eighth-grade children across ethnic groups has remained stagnant and there remains a persistent gap in achievement between White and Black and White and Hispanic eighth-grade students (National Assessment of Educational Progress, 2007).

In comparison to 44 other countries, most of which have lower rates of gross national income per capita, U.S. fourth graders perform in the middling range on significant measures of literacy achievement. In spite of the fact that the U.S. ranks in the top 25% of countries in terms of emphasis placed on reading in comparison to other subjects in schools, U.S. fourth graders rank 18th on measures of general reading achievement, 38th on measures of students' attitudes toward reading, 20th on students' reading self-concepts, and 31st on reading daily for fun outside of school (International Association for the Evaluation of Educational Achievement, 2007).

The last decade has seen a consensus around standards for high-quality reading instruction. The International Reading Association/National Association of the Education of Young Children produced standards that recommend instruction based around engaging stories, a balance of code instruction and meaningful activities, collaborative learning, individualized instruction, and engaging and challenging curriculum to expand world knowledge and vocabulary (1998). The National Reading Panel (2000) recommends that reading instruction emphasize phonemic awareness and phonics skills, reading comprehension strategies, vocabulary, and fluency. But curriculum in most schools remains teacher-directed, following traditional linear transmission modes of curriculum delivery (Olson, 2003), thus precluding the kind of learning specified in professional standards and policy. And the increasing fragmentation of competencies in the field of reading and the increasing reliance on scripted programs tied to specific testable goals, sometimes justified under the slogan of "what works" (Olson, 2004), overlooks the potential advantages of giving children the opportunity to explore for themselves the relationships between reading and writing as well as the relationships between literacy and basic oral competence (Olson, 2003; Olson & Torrance, 2009). After decades of effort, billions of dollars invested in scientifically based reading interventions, and sweeping initiatives to refine and implement such practices, U.S. literacy rates remain unimpressive. Innovation is justified.

Unison Reading is an alternative to conventional reading practices. The Unison Reading method is based on the logic of the social mind and goes something like this:

Y skill is underdeveloped in Student A. Provide Student A with access to a greater range of social groups in which Y skill is expressed. Opportunities to participate with others who possess Y skill will enable Student A to acquire Y skill and successfully perform Activity X. Unison Reading capitalizes on the special capacities that make us human—like having the ability to act out of empathy or to take another perspective. Collaboration and social interaction aren't mere marginal variables to what have come to be known as the *five pillars* of reading (vocabulary, fluency, phonics, phonemic awareness, and comprehension). Collaboration and social interaction are the very forces that provoke thinking through reading in the first place, bringing about occasions for using skills and strategies, and promoting achievement.

Jerome Bruner observed that Unison Reading is a form of consciousness raising in the domain of reading for both teachers and students (personal communication, February 17, 2010). The conception of reading instruction as *consciousness raising* is a way of broadening the focus of instruction away from a concern for teaching a narrow set of intramental skills toward a concern for enabling everyone—children as well as their teachers—to be more consciously aware of how reading functions as a form of social activity, one in which participants' intentions shape collective meaning. Unison Reading practices emphasize the many ways in which children take part as participants in literate ways of being and thinking through relationships with others in the context of reading activities.

Unison Reading forces the recognition that the social group is the very locus of new learning and instruction in the domain of reading. Group dialog is the medium of learning where children exercise their imagination, think creatively, express the occasional quirky ideas, and have fun, all the while exercising reading skills and competencies. Unison Reading borrows from Kenneth Gergen's social constructionist perspective to portray a "relational conception" of reading, emphasizing that relational ties are the locus of understanding (Gergen, 1990). In other words, the individual child's comprehension of a text can't be taken out of the context of the relationship(s) in which the text is interpreted. And since relationships are a medium of new understanding, they are a critical concern for pedagogy. Unison Reading places relational factors squarely at the center of concern in reading lessons.

Reading is a process that inherently relies on the human ability to think intersubjectively. And because of the human capacity to think intersubjectively, reading is a technological achievement that has shaped the course of humanity like none other. Children deserve a curriculum that approaches the subject of reading humanistically. The organization of this book has embraced this humanistic logic. It was my intention not to organize this book around the topical concerns that are typical of the reading instruction text genre such as *skills and competencies; grade levels or developmental levels; special students* (including English language learners and students with special needs); or *special topics* (like technology, gender, social justice). Rather, my intention was to offer a sufficiently broad conceptual framework for literacy as cultural practice and an aligning method of instruction that applies equally to all children. The point I tried to make is that all teachers of students of all levels are best served when they adhere to principles of literacy and learning that enable them to meet the needs of *all* children, regardless of developmental level, skill, special need, or circumstance.

■ A CONCLUDING STORY: UNISON READING AT THE JACOB RIIS SCHOOL

Unlike most reading interventions that are the invention of researchers and come into being outside of the classroom, Unison Reading came to life in a public school. And unlike conventional reading programs that adhere to the principles of general psychology, Unison Reading adheres to principles of equity and fairness and draws from social and cultural psychology as philosophical taproots. Unison Reading was tweaked and perfected through the countless trials presented through real-life classroom problems and dilemmas. Answers and solutions evolved as the practices were modified to target specific problems.

Throughout this book, I've introduced you to Kerry Rutishauser, the principal of 126, and many teachers at the school in order to illustrate Unison Reading practices. I'll end the book by telling you our collective story of Unison Reading and the impact it's had on the children of the Jacob Riis School.

Though the school is a cohesive community under the leadership of a single administration and leadership, it is actually comprised of two school populations. The elementary school, Primary School 126 (P.S. 126) serves children from the local neighborhood, including those who live in apartments within the public low-income housing project where the school is located and a portion of Chinatown, the port of entry for a large population of Chinese immigrants. Every year a small number of children enroll in the school after their families are assigned space in the homeless shelter adjacent to the school, and many of these children remain at the school even after the City finds housing in other boroughs. Almost 90% of children are from families who live below the poverty level.

The middle school, called the Manhattan Academy of Technology, is comprised of many children who matriculate from the elementary school as well as those who apply for admission from outside the school. The middle school is much more economically diverse than the elementary school, with a poverty rate under 50% and many children from very affluent households (see Figure 5.1 for comparative school census data).

If you imagine a snapshot of the over 750 children who attend The Jacob Riis School, you would see a kaleidoscope of traits in configurations common in many urban schools:

Figure 5.1   Jacob Riis School Census Data

K–5 School Census Data

Poverty

Free Meal	Reduced Meal	Full Meal
87.63%	6.18%	6.18%

Race

Asian	Hispanic	Black	White
57.6%	29%	10.5%	2.6%

Middle School Census Data

Poverty

Free Meal	Reduced Meal	Full Meal
48.99%	8.41%	42.61%

Race

Asian	Hispanic	Black	White
36.4%	22%	13.1%	29%

large numbers of children from single-parent households; a disproportionate level of emotional and behavioral disturbances; a disproportionate number of Black/African American and Hispanic/Latino children experience academic delays; high levels of linguistic diversity; large numbers of children who speak no English; and exposure to neighborhood violence and the lure of gang affiliation. Some children experience learning disabilities; others suffer emotional problems. With this composite image in mind, you might be questioning, like so many others who have become skeptical and impatient with the course of school reform: how much can schooling practices really do to assuage hardships of home circumstances or social injustices for children? How can children cross the barriers of race, class, and language in order to affiliate with and learn from one another in school when it is usually the instructional practices of schools themselves that sort and track students according to these categories?

A significant portion of the life of a child is spent within the walls of the school; what goes on there can make a huge difference in terms of how that child learns to view him or herself as a person whose life has meaning and potential. School should be a place that helps children overcome commonplace obstacles in order to achieve their potential, a goal that can only be accomplished through a curriculum that honors human potential. Unison Reading and the Genre Practice approach are founded upon the optimism of the democratic educational ideal. Schooling is still the best hope that children born into unfortunate circumstances have to overcome the conditions of birth and gain access to opportunities that can contribute to improved well-being. The Genre Practice curriculum exploits the culture of childhood, allowing independence, optimism, curiosity, resilience, humor, and playfulness to shape classroom interactions. The curriculum provides ample space in the school day for children to read, write, draw, and talk about topics of choice that are intrinsically appealing.

As with all children everywhere, the darker specks in the kaleidoscope of these children's lives are outshined by glints of joy, happiness, and hope. Children are enmeshed in extensive social networks of friends and family. Grandparents, aunts, uncles, cousins, sisters, brothers, and friends fill the children's lives with excitement, pleasure, and fun. The Jacob Riis School is a vibrant learning community, and each member is a valuable resource to others. The Genre Practice curriculum is designed to allow children to harness the rich resources of their lives.

I began working with Kerry and the faculty of The Jacob Riis School in the fall of 2007 as a literacy curriculum consultant responsible for K–8 writing staff development and immediately found myself amongst a community of educators who shared my commitments to educational practices that emphasized equity and engagement. I helped the staff learn to implement the Genre Practice writing instruction methods that I had developed. These practices emphasized the need for students to experience a sense of meaning and purpose in the curriculum, while also holding them accountable to high academic standards. With the success of the writing program, Kerry saw the benefits of adopting Genre Practice methods into the reading program, and asked me to train the teachers so that they could implement Unison Reading in all Pre-K–8 classrooms. The Unison Reading approach was introduced to teachers between January and April of 2009, and then mandated beginning in late April of 2009. In the fall of 2009, all teachers were expected to follow the approach to Unison Reading outlined in this book with every student, for the most part, being provided with two 15-minute Unison Reading sessions per week.

Kerry, the teachers, and I all forged ahead in implementing Unison Reading, believing in its potential to match or better the outcomes of the guided reading approach that had previously been used in the school. In order to monitor the students' progress and the efficacy of our instruction, we administer the Degrees of Reading Power assessment in the fall, winter, and spring of each academic year (Questar Assessment, 2000). As this book goes into production, the year-end DRP scores have come back, allowing us to make a comparative analysis of September and June scores and to make judgments about the efficacy of Unison Reading after a full-year period of schoolwide implementation. The average change in DRP units from September to June by grade level is featured in Table 5.2 together with national average gains in DRP units (special education and ELL student scores are included in these data).[1] Also featured are average changes in DRP units in children on each grade level who initially scored in the top and bottom 20% of the class (Figure 5.3 and 5.4 respectively). Figure 5.4 lists disaggregated DRP results for English language learners.

Though we were convinced the approach was sound, we did not anticipate the dramatic positive outcomes that were reflected in the progress-monitoring assessment results. Children in all grades exceeded the national annual rate of growth. Children in grades three, six, and seven doubled the national average gains. Children in fifth grade quadrupled the national average gains; and the average gains of children in eighth grade were five times greater than the national average. These gains were accomplished without expensive tiered interventions, increased emphasis on homework, pull-out programs for students, extensive skills work or test prep, additional tutoring, attention to leveling students and matching them with books, and without extensive professional development for teachers.[2] But some readers may still be skeptical. The first chapter of this book concluded with a list of questions commonly asked by teachers who are new to Unison Reading. These questions have been addressed in Chapters 2–4. But the achievement data presented here also speak directly to some of these questions, so I'll revisit them in light of year-end assessment results.

Is Unison Reading good for low-functioning readers? Aren't they embarrassed or frustrated? How do children with special needs or disabilities fare in Unison Reading groups? Changes in the scores of children who scored at opposite ends of the achievement spectrum were analyzed in order to determine how each group fared within the Unison Reading program. Children who initially scored in the bottom 20% of the DRP in September, due to a range of factors (learning disabilities, language acquisition/processing issues, mental functioning, for example) fared remarkably well during the year-long implementation of Unison Reading, outpacing the national annual average rate of growth at all grade levels. The average rate of growth in most

| Figure 5.2 | Jacob Riis Students' Average Gains in DRP Units Compared to National Average, September Through June, 2010 |

Grade	N of Students	Average Change in DRP Units, September–June	National Average Gain in DRP Units September–June*
2nd	57	+14.3	10
3rd	53	+15.9	8
4th	54	+9.5	6
5th	60	+13.4	3
6th	112	+8.8	4
7th	102	+6.9	3
8th	108	+11.0	2

Note: Scores are reported on a 100-point scale.

*Questar Assessment (2000).

[1]DRP test results were provided by Questar Assessment's Scoring and Reporting Services, and Questar staff provided support and verified the DRP gain score data analyses for accuracy.

[2]The total number of days per week the school outsourced literacy professional development services was reduced from 11 (worked by 5 consultants) in 2007–2008 to 2 in 2009–2010 as the school transitioned to the Genre Practice model.

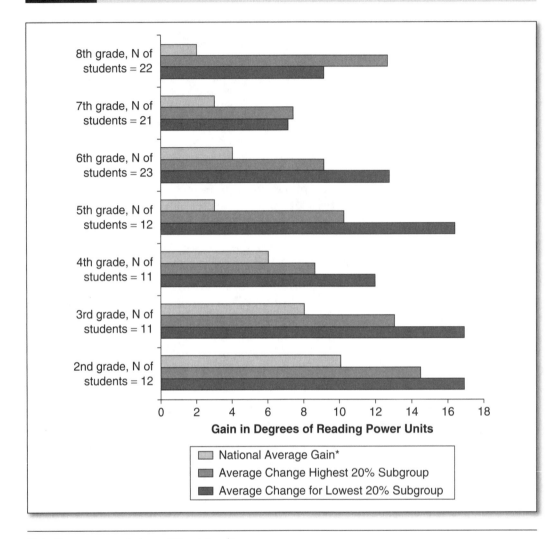

| Figure 5.3 | Students' Average Gains in DRP Units for Lowest 20% and Highest 20% Subgroups Compared to National Average Gains in DRP Units, September Through June, 2010 |

Note: Scores are reported on a 100-point scale.

*Questar Assessment (2000).

grades outpaced the national average rate of growth by multiples of two and three. The gains of the lowest-scoring 20% of fifth graders were five times greater than the national average, and lowest scoring 20% of eighth graders outpaced the national average by more than four times. The theory that children with particular needs fare best when they have access to groups of children who can compensate for these needs seems to be borne out by these data.

Is Unison Reading good for high-functioning readers? Aren't they bored? Don't they get frustrated by having to stop frequently and help their peers? Does time spent reading aloud detract from their opportunities to improve silent reading ability? Conventional wisdom suggests that learning opportunities for high-functioning students are diluted in mixed ability groups that include low-functioning students. The opposite is true. Opportunities to discuss what we know only sharpens and deepens our knowledge. The data on achievement patters for high-functioning readers bear out this theory. High-achieving students fared remarkably well in the integrated learning contexts of Unison Reading. The average gains achieved over the course of the year amongst the highest 20% of students exceeded the annual national average in all grades, and

Figure 5.4	English Language Learners Gains on the Degrees of Reading Power Assessment Compared to National Average Gains in DRP Units, September Through January

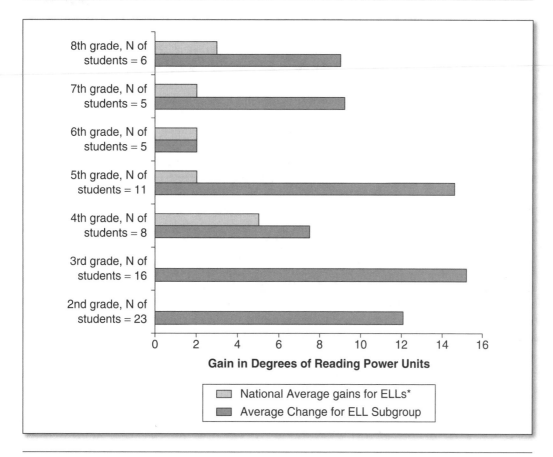

Note: Scores are reported on a 100-point scale.

*Maculaitis (2001).

in most grades doubled the national average. The highest scoring fifth-grade students outpaced the national average by more than three times, and the gains of the highest scoring eighth graders were six times greater than the national average. These data help dispel the common myth that "low" kids bring down the "high" kids in mixed ability groups.

What about ELLs? How can they participate if they don't speak English? Does their involvement in the group limit other children's learning opportunities? All children, including English language learners (ELLs), were assessed using the DRP, a test in English. After one year of Unison Reading, the average rate of growth of ELLs at all grade levels met or outpaced the national average. The average gains of ELLs in fifth grade was seven times greater than the national average. The average gains in seventh and eighth grade outpaced the national averages by rates of four and three respectively. The fact that these students achieved or even exceeded the national average growth levels affirms that Unison Reading enhances and improves achievement in reading for this population.

Our data tells a compelling story: Unison Reading, an approach that is engaging and fun for children, low cost, relatively easy to implement, and supportive of the development of teacher expertise has significantly improved levels of reading achievement within a large population of linguistically and culturally diverse children, the majority of whom live in poverty and come from homes with limited access to literacy.

■ CONCLUSION

At The Jacob Riis School, if you were to walk into any classroom at any grade level, you would see children taking part in reading groups that are integrated by race, class, gender, and ability. These "integrated" groups are a distinctive feature of Unison Reading, and contribute to important facets of children's learning. The organization of these groups is uniform—no more than five children join together in an oral, synchronized reading of a joint text as they follow a few simple rules: Read loudly enough so that others can hear you (but not so loudly that your voice overpowers), keep pace with one another, stop the group and speak up when you are confused or have something to say that others might benefit from hearing, and act in ways that promote others' learning. Each week a few group leaders are responsible for selecting a text that a few of their classmates will then sign up to read. Groups meet several times over the course of the week, and then the whole process begins again the following week, and the week after that, and the one after that . . . Over the course of the year, everyone has the opportunity to read 30–40 different texts of their choosing, all of which involve some level of teacher-facilitated instruction. Children use the format of Unison Reading to deliberate over comics, gossip columns, sports articles, history and science texts, and math problems. Unison Reading carves out social space across grade levels and content areas for children to insinuate the spoken word into their reading of the printed word.

Unison Reading "works" on several levels. On one level, Unison Reading supports vocabulary, fluency, phonics, and comprehension development because group reading situations require children to exercise these cognitive operations. Children voice their own confusions aloud to others at the table, and tablemates "follow in" to the point of confusion. Instruction is ultra explicit because the locus of instruction stems from children's confusions at the moment of need rather than points predetermined by the teacher. Thus, Unison Reading interactions are pedagogically much more powerful than traditional teacher-directed instructional formats where children are expected to follow into the teacher's focus of attention (which many children have difficulty doing).

With an emphasis on learning rather than teaching, instruction is inherently "developmentally appropriate" because children themselves bring attention to points in the text that cause cognitive dissonance. Indeed, Unison Reading helps prevent teaching from interfering with learning.

But Unison Reading also "works" on another level that has been woefully neglected by the field of reading specifically and by the traditions of formal education in general. Unison Reading provides opportunities for children to take part in "conjoint communicated experience," which John Dewey deemed vital to democratic society (1944). The Unison Reading protocol scaffolds the group experience so that children with varying levels of reading skill and sociocognitive and socioperceptual competence can participate to maintain their own cohesive groups. Throughout the course of the year, children have opportunities to participate in over 40 different Unison Reading groups, experiences that help enhance their multicontextual competencies, or the ability to move flexibly into different social groups. In Unison Reading groups, children not only learn how to read, they learn how to live socially. Unison Reading invites children to act of their own volition to take part in a process of collective reading of texts that address topics they care about in groups that are not restrictive on the basis of achievement status. Unison Reading is a pedagogy of personal responsibility and autonomy and provides children opportunities to cultivate the intentions befitting citizens of a free democracy, such as the rights and responsibilities of free expression. Because children have opportunities to act on issues of personal concern, to deliberate the merits of their ideas, and to broaden their perspectives in the company of others, they learn how to participate in civil discourse, arguably the most fundamental goal of reading education in a democracy.

Afterword

I resonate to the notion advanced by Michael Martinez, who argues for "Education as the cultivation of intelligence" (Martinez, 2000). For several years now I have been concerned that we, educators, are sometimes so preoccupied with helping students to learn the content and skills that we teach, that we neglect to give attention to the development of the disposition and the adaptive capacity to use what we teach to solve human problems. I have come to the conclusion that pedagogy should be about the use of academic content and skills to enhance the development of adaptive abilities so that the teaching of the sciences, mathematics or reading, as examples, is as a means rather than the end.

How refreshing it is to find a student of the teaching of reading who shares this perspective. Cynthia McCallister's *Unison Reading* shows us that the teaching and learning of reading can result in the cultivation of *humane* intelligence. *Unison Reading* is much more than a book about how to teach reading, it is a book about the teaching and learning of reading with the intent to humanize the adaptive abilities of learning persons. The title *Unison Reading* captures an intriguing instructional process, but the title does not do justice to the potential of the method to accommodate the intentionality of teaching and learning transactions and to bring them into central focus in the cultivation of intelligence.

One usually teaches with the intent that others learn. The intent of the teaching and learning behavior may not always be so explicit. Some of what is learned may be incidental or accidental, but the teaching and learning are seldom without purpose. McCallister makes her teaching of reading intentionally multi-purposive and, in the process, transforms the teaching of reading into the teaching and learning of humane living. In the process of learning to live one's life humanely, one learns the skill of deriving meaning from organized graphic symbols. To derive meaning requires more than simple decoding and translation. To achieve meaning and understanding one must think about and adjudicate relations between disparate phenomena. Unison Reading recognizes that relational adjudication is both social and intentional. Thus the teaching and learning processes are intentional and social. The intent is bi-focal: to learn to read and to learn to be humanely adaptive. The instrumental process is social.

The construct of intentionality received some attention from the field of psychology in the closing years of the 19th century. However, intentionality proved to be highly subjective, situation sensitive, and hostile to validation. The construct did not gain traction in the behavioral sciences, which were modeled on the natural sciences. Likewise, intentionality has not emerged as a salient construct in the sciences of pedagogy. Despite the fact that it is difficult to ignore intentionality and purpose in teaching and learning, except as reflected in the goals of education or the objectives of the curriculum, intentionality has not emerged as a prominent concern in teaching and learning. When intentionality has been the focus of attention, educators have tended to be constrained by declared intent as purpose—to teach or learn how to read; to teach another to be a critical thinker; or to master instrumental academic skills. In Cultural Psychology intentionality connotes things that have no natural reality. Rather, a phenomenon achieves intentionality because "its existence is real, factual, and forceful, but only so long as there is a community of persons whose beliefs, desires, emotions, purposes, and other mental representations are directed at it, and are thereby influenced by it. . . . Intentional worlds do not exist independent of the intentional states (beliefs, desires, emotions, etc.) directed at them, by persons who live in them" (Shweder, 1990, p. 2).

Through *Unison Reading* McCallister recognizes these intentional worlds and guides the teaching and learning experiences of learning persons in these worlds as these individuals (in this case, K–8 students) constitute themselves. They live in intentional worlds and use them to advance their learning of reading and their broader development. McCallister's work brings the intentional worlds of teaching and learning transactions into central focus, and provides clinical evidence of what can happen in classrooms. On the conceptual frame provided by intentionality, McCallister imposes such humane values as democratic processes, fairness, social justice, social inclusion and human agency, all of which are compatible with intentionality—but none are essential to the construct, except that once the social nature of human enterprise is privileged, pro-social values must follow. Reading is a social as well as a cognitive skill. McCallister has brilliantly combined the teaching of both through *Unison Reading*.

Edmund W. Gordon

John M. Musser Professor of Psychology,
Emeritus—Yale University

Richard March Hoe Professor of Psychology and Education,
Emeritus—Teachers College, Columbia University

Appendix A

Unison Reading Record

Title: _____ Genre Form: _____ Date: _____

	SOCIAL PROCESSES (SP)		**GENRE (G)**

Unison Reading Rules   Coordinating Behaviors

Pacing—Fluency, Expression, and Prosody   Reading in Sync

Affective Factors (attitude/attention/engagement/motivation)

Relational and Interpersonal Factors (resolving conflict/showing promotive behaviors)

Text Form and Purpose   Genre Conventions

Syntax and Grammar   Punctuation

Layout, Text Features   Reader Stance (customs of reading text form)

COMPREHENSION (C)

Predict

Evaluate

Summarize

Infer, Draw Conclusions

Prior Knowledge

Question

Synthesize

Create Images

Vocabulary

Interpretation (Fluency/Expression/Punctuation)

DECODING AND STRATEGIC PROCESSING (D)

Strategy Use (rereading/looking back, self-monitoring, self-correcting, cros checking, reading ahead, punctuation)

Phonics (blending and segmenting, letter-sound correspondence, word families, grapheme/phoneme relationships, onset/rime)

Word Reading Strategies (contextual analysis; morphological relationships; relating known words to unknown words)

Record **BREACHES** in order of occurrence

CODE/ Breach	Teacher	Student 1	Student 2	Student 3	Student 4	Student 5	Record INSTRUCTIONAL POINT that follows in to corresponding breach or insight
#1							
#2							
#3							
#4							

Unison Reading Record

Title: _____ Genre Form: _____ Date: _____

Record **BREACHES** in order of occurrence

CODE/ Breach	Teacher	Student 1	Student 2	Student 3	Student 4	Student 5	Record INSTRUCTIONAL POINT that follows in to corresponding breach or insight
#							
#							
#							
#							
#							
#							

124

Unison Reading Analysis

Total Breaches	
Social Processes	%
Genre	%
Comprehension	%
Decoding	%

Members	% Participated	% Breached

Instructional Inventory

Social Processes	Genre	Comprehension	Decoding

Instructional Inventory, continued . . .

Social Processes	Genre	Comprehension	Decoding

Instructional Priority List

List children's names in order of priority as determined by diagnostic assessment score.

First-Level Students	SCORE	Second-Level Students	SCORE
1		6	
2		7	
3		8	
4		9	
5		10	

Third-Level Students	SCORE	Fourth-Level Students	SCORE
11		16	
12		17	
13		18	
14		19	
15		20	

Fifth-Level Students	SCORE	Sixth-Level Students	SCORE
21		26	
22		27	
23		28	
24		29	
25		30	

Student Unison Reading Log

Name: _____ Date:_____

Text Title: _____ Genre: _____

Group Leader	Member #1	Member #2	Member #3	Member #4	Member #5

Unison Reading Rules: Remember to read in sync with the others; read audibly so others can hear you; speak up when you're confused by a word or an idea; be helpful and supportive to group members.

Every time you meet with your group, be thoughtful about your accomplishments and goals. Record the most important ones.'

Date:	Date:	Date:	Date:
Accomplishment:	Accomplishment:	Accomplishment:	Accomplishment:
Goal:	Goal:	Goal:	Goal:

Think bigger: What was the most important big idea you took from your reading? Can you write a question that this idea answered?

Big idea:

Big question:

Unison Reading Word Work

Mystery Word	What does it mean?	How did I learn the meaning?

Unison Reading Rubric

Behaviors are rated on a scale of 1–3, described below:

1: Behaviors are under developed, rarely observed, or developed to an unsatisfactory degree.

2: Behaviors are occasionally observed, but need to be developed.

3: Behaviors are well established and secured in group process and instructional practice.

Group Process	Rating
Students contribute to dialog: Students assume responsibility for following into one another's comments	
Students identify points of confusion by initiating the majority of breaches	
Teacher serves facilitative role: Teachers follow into comments and confusions only after students themselves have had sufficient opportunity to resolve confusion	
Students control dialog: Group process supports evidence that students, and not the teacher, routinely control the course of dialog within reading groups	
Students manage the group process: Students utilize the rules of Unison Reading to address group process *and* reading process concerns	
Students demonstrate promotive behaviors toward their peers	
Students demonstrate metacognitive awareness: Students are able to recognize when understanding breaks down and readily breach the group in such instances	
Contributions to dialog are evenly distributed: Students demonstrate an appreciation for the importance of shared dialog by neither dominating conversation nor refraining from participation	
Independence: Children are able to meet independently of a teacher and still maintain coherent groups (they can resolve conflict and misunderstanding with relative independence)	
Instructional scaffolding: Teacher resolves confusion and elaborates understanding when necessary	
Wrap up: Teacher facilitates debrief during final few minutes of group, helping children identify accomplishments and goals	

Recordkeeping

Recordkeeping skill: Teacher demonstrates facility in recording summaries of student discourse	
Instructional analysis: Teacher is able to assess the conversation initiated after the breach to identify instructional points addressed and to code breaches under appropriate reading domains	
Instructional sufficiency: Records provide evidence that teachers meet each group on a twice-weekly basis and/or that teachers meet with groups twice a day	
Instructional quality: Records show evidence that a full range of instructional points emerge and get addressed through group dialog	
Large-group instruction: Evidence that insights gained from teacher's involvement in Unison Reading groups informs large-group lesson content	

Classroom Procedures and Organization

Procedures are established to support group leaders in making and posting text selections	
Procedures are in place for children to sign up for groups of their choice on a fair and consistent basis	
Evidence of a consistent system for distributed group leadership—the role of group leader rotates weekly so that students have equal and frequent opportunities to assume the role of group leader	
Student independence: Children demonstrate independence in gathering for groups, initiating reading process, and quickly becoming engaged in independent work after group meetings conclude	
Student recordkeeping: Students complete logs after group session concludes	
Space and materials: Teachers meet with their groups at a small table cleared of all materials but text photocopies, a white board, and marker (for word work)	

Appendix B

Fourth-Grade Genre Practice Standards Checklist for Instructional Accounting

Topic   *Date Taught*

Reading Standards: Literature (RL)

Key Ideas and Details

1. Refer to details and examples in a text when explaining what the text says explicitly and when drawing inferences from the text.				
2. Determine a theme of a story, drama, or poem from details in the text; summarize the text.				
3. Describe in depth a character, setting, or event in a story or drama, drawing on specific details in the text (e.g., a character's thoughts, words, or actions).				

Craft and Structure

4. Determine the meaning of words and phrases as they are used in a text, including those that allude to significant characters found in mythology (e.g., Herculean).				
5. Explain major differences between poems, drama, and prose, and refer to the structural elements of poems (e.g., verse, rhythm, meter) and drama (e.g., casts of characters, settings, descriptions, dialogue, stage directions) when writing or speaking about a text.				
6. Compare and contrast the point of view from which different stories are narrated, including the difference between first- and third-person narrations.				

Integration of Knowledge and Ideas

7. Make connections between the text of a story or drama and a visual or oral presentation of the text, identifying where each version reflects specific descriptions and directions in the text.				
8. (Not applicable to literature)				
9. Compare and contrast the treatment of similar themes and topics (e.g., opposition of good and evil) and patterns of events (e.g., the quest) in stories, myths, and traditional literature from different cultures.				

Range of Reading and Complexity of Text

10. By the end of the year, read and comprehend literature, including stories, dramas, and poetry, in the grades 4–5 text complexity band proficiently, with scaffolding as needed at the high end of the range.				

eading Standards: Informational Texts (RI)

ey Ideas and Details

1. Refer to details and examples in a text when explaining what the text says explicitly and when drawing inferences from the text.				
2. Determine the main idea of a text and explain how it is supported by key details; summarize the text.				
3. Explain events, procedures, ideas, or concepts in a historical, scientific, or technical text, including what happened and why, based on specific information in the text.				

raft and Structure

4. Determine the meaning of general academic and domain-specific words or phrases in a text relevant to a *grade 4 topic or subject area.*				
5. Describe the overall structure (e.g., chronology, comparison, cause/effect, problem/solution) of events, ideas, concepts, or information in a text or part of a text.				
6. Compare and contrast a firsthand and secondhand account of the same event or topic; describe the differences in focus and the information provided.				

ntegration of Knowledge and Ideas

7. Interpret information presented visually, orally, or quantitatively (e.g., in charts, graphs, diagrams, time lines, animations, or interactive elements on Web pages) and explain how the information contributes to an understanding of the text in which it appears.				
8. Explain how an author uses reasons and evidence to support particular points in a text.				
9. Integrate information from two texts on the same topic in order to write or speak about the subject knowledgeably.				

Range of Reading and Level of Text Complexity

10. By the end of the year, read and comprehend informational texts, including history/social studies, science, and technical texts, in the grades 4–5 text complexity band proficiently, with scaffolding as needed at the high end of the range.				

Reading Standards: Foundational Skills (RF)

Print Concepts

NA

Phonological Awareness

NA

Phonics and Word Recognition

3. Know and apply grade-level phonics and word analysis skills in decoding words.				
Use combined knowledge of all letter-sound correspondences, syllabication patterns, and morphology (e.g., roots and affixes) to read accurately unfamiliar multisyllabic words in context and out of context.				

Fluency

4. Read with sufficient accuracy and fluency to support comprehension.				
Read on-level text with purpose and understanding.				
Read on-level prose and poetry orally with accuracy, appropriate rate, and expression on successive readings.				
Use context to confirm or self-correct word recognition and understanding, rereading as necessary.				

Speaking and Listening Standards (SL)

Comprehension and Collaboration

1. Engage effectively in a range of collaborative discussions (one-on-one, in groups, and teacher-led) with diverse partners on *grade 4 topics and texts*, building on others' ideas and expressing their own clearly.				
Come to discussions prepared, having read or studied required material; explicitly draw on that preparation and other information known about the topic to explore ideas under discussion.				
Follow agreed-upon rules for discussions and carry out assigned roles.				
Pose and respond to specific questions to clarify or follow up on information, and make comments that contribute to the discussion and link to the remarks of others.				
Review the key ideas expressed and explain their own ideas and understanding in light of the discussion.				
2. Paraphrase portions of a text read aloud or information on presented in diverse media and formats, including visually, quantitatively, and orally.				
3. Identify the reasons and evidence a speaker provides to support particular points.				

Presentation of Knowledge and Ideas

4. Report on a topic or text, tell a story, or recount an experience in an organized manner, using appropriate facts and relevant, descriptive details to support main ideas or themes; speak clearly at an understandable pace.				
5. Add audio recordings and visual displays to presentations when appropriate to enhance the development of main ideas or themes.				
6. Differentiate between contexts that call for formal English (e.g., presenting ideas) and situations where informal discourse is appropriate (small-group discussion); use formal English when appropriate to task and situation.				

Recommended Children's Magazines

Grades K–2		
Your Big Backyard	www.nwf.org/YourBigBackyard	Created by the National Wildlife Federation, this magazine explores the wonders of nature and its inhabitants through wildlife poetry, fiction, crafts, games, and puzzles.
National Geographic Kids, National Geographic Little Kids	http://kids.nationalgeographic.com/	An interactive magazine that includes science, geography, technology, wildlife, and current event articles as well as games, puzzles, comics, and activities.
Scholastic News	http://teacher.scholastic.com/products/classmags/sn1.htm	A social studies magazine that features nonfiction articles, activities, and materials to develop children's literacy skills.
Spider	http://www.cobblestonepub.com/magazine/SDR/	A magazine with stories, riddles, poems, and nonfiction articles chosen to encourage children to become creative, independent readers with critical thinking skills.
Time for Kids	http://www.timeforkids.com/	A current events magazine that includes real-world topics, national news, and a "Cartoon of the Week" feature to motivate kids to read.
Zoobooks	http://www.zoobooks.com/	A colorful animal magazine that features fascinating animals, birds, and insects, with puzzles, games, and activities.
Zootles	http://www.zoobooks.com/	An animal magazine for prereaders and beginning readers that explores wildlife, animal facts, and games, incorporating beginning literacy skills and problem-solving activities.

Grades 3–5		
American Girl	http://www.americangirl.com/	An age-appropriate alternative to teen magazines, this magazine for girls features stories, crafts, quizzes, advice, games, and poems.
Ask	http://www.cobblestonepub.com/magazine/ASK/	A science magazine that features contemporary and past inventors, artists, and scientists and explores their contributions with enlightening articles, activities, and puzzles.

References

Alexander, R., Armstrong, M., Flutter, J., Hargreaves, L., Harrison, D., et al. (2009). *Children, their world, their education: Final report and recommendations of the Cambridge primary review.* London, UK: Routledge.

American Psychiatric Association. (2000). *Diagnostic and Statistical Manual of Mental Disorders* (4th ed.). Washington, DC: Author.

Annon, K. (2009). *Literacy: 'A prerequisite for peace.'* Retrieved August 16, 2010, from http://www.un .org/News/Press/docs/2002/sgsm8353.doc.htm

Astington, J. W., Harris, P. L., & Olson, D. R. (Eds.). (1988). *Developing theories of mind.* Cambridge, UK: Cambridge University Press.

Bakhtin, M. M., Holquist, M., & Emerson, C. (1986). *Speech genres and other late essays.* Austin: University of Texas Press.

Benedict, R. (1934). *Patterns of culture.* New York: Mentor Books.

Block, C. C., & Parris, S. R. (2008). Using neuroscience to inform reading comprehension instruction. In C. C. Block & S. R. Parris (Eds.), *Comprehension Instruction: Research-based best practices* (2nd ed., pp. 114–126). New York: Guilford Press.

Block, C. C., Parris, S. R., & Whiteley, C. S. (2008). CPMs: A kinesthetic comprehension strategy. *The Reading Teacher, 61*(6), 440–448.

Board of Education of the City of New York. (1997). New Standards™ Performance Standards *for English Language Arts* (1st New York City ed.). New York: Author.

Bruner, J. (1982). Formats of language acquisition. *American Journal of Semiotics, 1,* 1–16.

Bruner, J. (1983). *Child's talk.* New York: Norton.

Bruner, J. (1996). *The culture of education.* Cambridge, MA: Harvard University Press.

Carver, C. S., & Scheier, M. F. (2005). Engagement, disengagement, coping and catastrophe. In A. Elliot & C. Dweck (Eds.), *Handbook of competence and motivation* (pp. 527–547). New York: Guilford Press.

Clark, T. (2009, September). *Integrating the first-grade classroom.* Paper presented at Unison Reading and Classroom Desegregation Conference, New York, NY.

Clay, M. (1991). *Becoming literate: The construction of inner control.* Portsmouth, NH: Heinemann.

Clay, M. M. (2002). *An observation survey: Of early literacy achievement* (2nd ed.). Auckland, NZ: Heinemann.

Daniels, H. (2002). *Literature circles: Voice and choice in book clubs and reading groups* (2nd ed.). Portland, ME: Stenhouse Publishers.

Deci, E. L., & Ryan, R. M. (1985). *Intrinsic motivation and self-determination in human behavior.* New York: Plenum.

Deci, E. L., & Ryan, R. M. (2002). *Handbook of self-determination research.* Rochester, NY: University of Rochester Press.

Deci, E. L., & Moller, A. C. (2005). The concept of competence: A starting place for understanding intrinsic motivation and self-determined extrinsic motivation. In A. J. Elliott & C. S. Dweck (Eds.), *Handbook of competence and motivation* (pp. 579–597). New York: Guilford Press.

Dehaene, S. (2009). *Reading in the brain.* New York: Viking.

Delpit, L. (1986). Skills and other dilemmas of a progressive Black educator. *Harvard Educational Review, 56*(4), 379–385.

Dewey, J. (1944). *Democracy and education.* New York: Free Press.

Dunbar, R. I. M. (1998). The social brain hypothesis. *Evolutionary Anthropology, 6*(5), 178–190.

Dweck, C. (2006). *Self-theories: Their role in motivation, personality, and development.* Philadelphia: Psychology Press/Taylor & Francis.

Fountas, I. C., & Pinnell, G. S. (1996). *Guided reading: Good first teaching for all children.* Portsmouth, NH: Heinemann.

Gambrell, L. B., Malloy, J. A., & Mazzoni, S. A. (2007). Evidence-based best practices for comprehensive literacy instruction. In L. B. Gambrell, L. M. Morrow, M. Pressley, & J. T. Guthrie (Eds.), *Best practices in literacy instruction* (3rd ed., pp. 11–29). New York: Guilford Press.

Gamse, B. C., Jacob, R. T., Horst, M., Boulay, B., & Unlu, F. (2008). *Reading first impact study final report* (NCEE 2009–4038). Washington, DC: National Center for Education Evaluation and Regional Assistance, Institute of Education Sciences, U.S. Department of Education.

Gergen, K. (1990). Social understanding and the inscription of self. In J. Stigler, R. Shweder, & G. Herdt (Eds.), *Cultural psychology: Essays on comparative human development* (pp. 470–606). New York: Cambridge University Press.

Goldberg, E. (2009). *The new executive brain: Frontal lobes in a complex world.* New York: Oxford University Press.

Goodman, K. S. (1967). Reading: A psycholinguistic guessing game. *Journal of the Reading Specialist, 6*(4), 126–135.

Gordon, E. (1999). *Education and justice: A view from the back of the bus.* New York: Teachers College Press.

Grice, P. (1989). *Studies in the way of words.* Cambridge, MA: Harvard University Press.

Hemphill, L., & Snow, C. (1996). Language and literacy development: Discontinuities and differences. In D. R. Olson & N. Torrance (Eds.), *The handbook of education and human development* (pp. 173–201). Cambridge, MA: Blackwell.

Holdaway, D. (1979). *The foundations of literacy.* New York: Ashton Scholastic.

International Association for the Evaluation of Educational Achievement. (2007). *PIRLS 2006 Technical Report.* Boston: TIMSS & PIRLS International Study Center, Lynch School of Education, Boston College.

Johnson, D., Johnson, R., & Holubec, E. (1994). *The new circles of learning: Cooperation in the classroom and school.* Alexandria, VA: Association of Supervision and Curriculum Development.

Keene, E., & Zimmerman, S. (1997). *Mosaic of thought: Teaching comprehension in a reader's workshop.* Portsmouth, NH: Heinemann.

Klinkenborg, V. (2009, March 16). Some thoughts on the lost art of reading aloud. *NY Times Editorial Observer.* Retrieved July 15, 2009, from http://www.nytimes.com/2009/05/16/opinion/16sat4.html

Kuhn, M. R., & Rasinski, T. (2007). Best practices in fluency instruction. In L. B. Gambrell, L. M. Morrow, M. Pressley, & J. T. Guthrie (Eds.), *Best practices in literacy instruction* (3rd ed., pp. 204–219). New York: Guilford Press.

Lennon, C., & Burdick, H. (2004). *The Lexile framework as an approach for reading measurement and success (The Lexile framework for reading white paper).* Durham, NC: MetaMetrics.

Lleras, C., & Rangel, C. (2009). Ability grouping practices in elementary school and African American/Hispanic achievement. *American Journal of Education, 115*(2), 279–304.

Maculaitis, J. (2001). *The MAC II handbook with norms tables: A & B forms.* Brewster, NY: Questar Assessment.

Martinez, M. E. (2000). *Education as the cultivation of intelligence.* Mahwah, NJ: Lawrence Erlbaum Publishers.

National Assessment of Educational Progress. (2002). *Oral reading fluency scale.* Retrieved August 16, 2010, from http://nces.ed.gov/nationsreportcard/studies/ors/scale.asp.

National Center on Education and the Economy and the University of Pittsburgh. (1997). *New performance standards.* New York: Board of Education of the City of New York.

National Reading Panel. (2000). *Teaching children to read: An evidence-based assessment of the scientific research literature on reading and its implications for reading instruction.* Bethesda, MD: National Institute of Child Health and Human Development.

Northwest Evaluation Association. (2003). *Measures of academic progress.* Retrieved August 11, 2010, from http://www.nwea.org/products-services/computer-based-adaptive-assessments/map

Olson, D. R. (2003). *Psychological theory and educational reform: How school remakes mind and society.* New York: Cambridge University Press.

Olson, D. R. (2004). The triumph of hope over experience in the search for "What works": A response to Slavin. *Educational Researcher, 33,* 24–26.

Olson, D. R. (2007). Self-ascription of intention: Responsibility, obligation and self-control. *Synthese, 159*(2), 297–314.

Olson, D. R. (2009a). Literacy, literacy policy, and the school. In D. R. Olson & N. Torrance. (Eds.), *The Cambridge handbook of literacy* (pp. 556–576). New York: Cambridge University Press.

Olson, D. R. (2009b). Language, literacy and mind: The literacy hypothesis. *Psykhe, 18*(1), 3–9.

Olson, D. R., & Torrance, N. (Eds.). *The Cambridge handbook of literacy.* New York: Cambridge University Press.

Palincsar, A. S., & Brown, A. L. (1984). Reciprocal teaching of comprehension—Fostering and monitoring activities. *Cognition and Instruction, 1,* 117–175.

Pearson, P. D. & Gallagher, M. (1983). The instruction of reading comprehension. *Contemporary Educational Psychology, 8,* 317–344.

Peterson, R., & Eeds, M. (1990). *Grand conversations: Literature groups in action.* New York: Scholastic.

Pressley, M. (2000). What should comprehension instruction be the instruction of? In M. L. Kamil, P. B. Mosenthal, P. D. Pearson, & R. Barr (Eds.), *Handbook of reading research: Volume III* (pp. 545–561). Mahwah, NJ: Lawrence Erlbaum.

Questar Assessment. (2000). *DRP norms: Primary and standard DRP test forms.* Brewster, NY: Author. Retrieved August 15, 2010, from http://www.QuestarAI.com/products/drpprogram

Rasinski, T.V. (2004). *Assessing reading fluency.* Honolulu, HI: Pacific Resources for Education and Learning.

Rawls, J. (1999). *A theory of justice* (2nd ed.). Cambridge: Harvard University Press.

Ricketts, J., Nation, K., & Bishop, D. V. M. (2007). Vocabulary is important for some, but not all reading skills. *Scientific Studies of Reading, 11,* 235–257.

Rizzolatti, G., & Craighero, L. (2004). The mirror-neuron system. *Annual Review of Neuroscience, 27,* 169–192.

Rylant, C. (1985). Slower than the rest. In C. Rylant (Ed.), *Every living thing* (pp. 1–7). New York: Aladdin Paperbacks.

Sapir, E. (1932). Cultural anthropology and psychiatry. *The Journal of Abnormal and Social Psychology, 27*(3), 229–242.

Scholastic. (2006). Scholastic reading inventory (SRI). Retrieved July 20, 2010, from http://teacher.scholastic.com/products/sri/

Shweder, R. A. (1990). Cultural psychology—What is it? In J. W. Stigler, R. A. Shweder, & G. S. Herdt (Eds.), *Cultural Psychology: Essays on Comparative Human Development* (pp. 1–43). Cambridge, UK: Cambridge University Press.

Share, D. L. (2008). On the Anglocentricities of current reading research and practice: The perils of overreliance on an "outlier" orthography. *Psychological Bulletin, 134*(4), 584–615.

Stone, V. (2000). The role of the frontal lobes and the amygdala in theory of mind. In S. Baron-Cohen, H. Tager-Flusberg, & D. J. Cohen (Eds.), *Understanding other minds: Perspectives from developmental cognitive neuroscience* (pp. 253–273). Oxford: Oxford University Press.

Tager-Flusberg, H. & Sullivan, K. (2000). A componential theory of mind: Evidence from Williams' syndrome. *Cognition, 76,* 59–89.

University of Oregon Center on Teaching and Learning. (n.d.). *DIBELS Data System.* Retrieved October 12, 2010, from https://dibels.uoregon.edu/

Yalom, I. D. (2005). *The theory and practice of group psychotherapy.* (5th ed.). New York: Basic Books.

Index

Note: Numbers in *italics* refer to forms.

CORWIN

A SAGE Company

The Corwin logo—a raven striding across an open book—represents the union of courage and learning. Corwin is committed to improving education for all learners by publishing books and other professional development resources for those serving the field of PreK–12 education. By providing practical, hands-on materials, Corwin continues to carry out the promise of its motto: **"Helping Educators Do Their Work Better."**